FUNDAMENTALS OF
English
Grammar
FOURTH EDITION

FUNDAMENTALS OF
English
Grammar

FOURTH EDITION

VOLUME B with Essential Online Resources

Betty S. Azar
Stacy A. Hagen

Fundamentals of English Grammar, Fourth Edition
Volume B

Azar Associates: Shelley Hartle, Editor, and Sue Van Etten, Manager

Pearson Education, 221 River Street, Hoboken, NJ 07030

Staff credits: The people who made up the *Fundamentals of English Grammar, Fourth Edition* team, representing editorial, production, design, and manufacturing, are, Dave Dickey, Christine Edmonds, Ann France, Amy McCormick, Robert Ruvo, and Ruth Voetmann.

Text composition: S4Carlisle Publishing Services

Illustrations: Don Martinetti—pages 216, 217, 219, 224, 230, 232, 234, 242, 244, 245, 250, 253, 254, 258, 263, 266, 277, 278, 292, 299, 300, 304, 305, 308, 309, 313, 327, 344, 347, 349, 356, 364, 373, 374, 385, 386; Chris Pavely—pages 213, 227, 229, 231, 233, 260, 268, 275, 276, 281, 319, 322, 331, 337, 338, 360, 363, 377, 386, 389, 391, 392

Printed in the United States of America

ISBN 10: 0-13-466110-9
ISBN 13: 978-0-13-466110-0

To my sister, Jo

B.S.A.

For D. P. and H. B.
with appreciation

S.H.

Contents

Preface to the Fourth Edition

Fundamentals of English Grammar is a developmental skills text for lower-intermediate and intermediate English language learners. It uses a grammar-based approach integrated with communicative methodologies to promote the development of all language skills in a variety of ways. Starting from a foundation of understanding form and meaning, students engage in meaningful communication about real actions, real things, and their real lives in the classroom context. *Fundamentals of English Grammar* functions principally as a classroom teaching text but also serves as a comprehensive reference text for students and teachers.

The eclectic approach and abundant variety of exercise material remain the same as in the earlier editions, but this fourth edition incorporates new ways and means. In particular:

- **WARM-UP EXERCISES FOR THE GRAMMAR CHARTS**
  Newly created for the fourth edition, these innovative exercises precede the grammar charts and introduce the point(s) to be taught. They have been carefully crafted to help students *discover* the target grammar as they progress through each warm-up exercise.

- **LISTENING PRACTICE**
  Numerous listening exercises help students interact with the spoken language in a variety of settings that range from the relaxed, casual speech of everyday conversation to more academic content. The student text audio is available on Essential Online Resources, and a full listening script can be found in the back of the book.

- **READINGS**
  Students can read and respond to a wide selection of readings that focus on the target grammar structure(s).

- **WRITING TASKS**
  New writing activities that practice target structures have been created for every chapter. A writing sample precedes each task so students have a model to follow.

- **EXPANDED SPEAKING ACTIVITIES**
  Students have even more opportunities to share their experiences, express their opinions, and relate the target grammar to their personal lives. The text often uses the students' own life experiences as context and regularly introduces topics of interest to stimulate the free expression of ideas in structured as well as open discussions.

- **CORPUS-INFORMED CONTENT**
  Based on our corpus research, grammar content has been added, deleted, or modified to reflect the discourse patterns of spoken and written English.

Components of Fundamentals of English Grammar, Fourth Edition:

- **Student Book with Essential Online Resources** includes the access code for the audio, self-assessments, and teacher resources with the Student Book answer key.
- **Student Book with MyEnglishLab** that includes the access code to MyEnglishLab, an easy-to-use online learning management system that delivers rich online practice to engage and motivate students.
- A comprehensive ***Workbook,*** consisting of self-study exercises for independent work.
- An all-new ***Teacher's Guide,*** with step-by-step teaching suggestions for each chart, notes to the teacher on key grammar structures, vocabulary lists, and expansion activities and *PowerPoint* presentations for key chapters.
- An expanded ***Test Bank,*** with additional quizzes, chapter tests, and mid-term and final exams.
- ***Test-Generator*** software that allows teachers to customize their own tests using quizzes and tests from the *Test Bank.*
- ***PowerPoint*** presentations for key chapters. Based on real-world readings, these lessons are designed for use in the classroom as "beyond-the-book" activities. They can be found in the new *Teacher's Guide* or downloaded from *AzarGrammar.com.*
- A ***Chartbook,*** a reference book consisting only of the grammar charts.
- ***AzarGrammar.com,*** a website that provides a variety of supplementary classroom materials and a place where teachers can support each other by sharing their knowledge and experience.

MyEnglishLab

MyEnglishLab provides a range of interactive activities that help motivate and engage students. MyEnglishLab for *Fundamentals of English Grammar,* Fourth Edition includes:

- Rich online practice for all skill areas: grammar, reading, writing, speaking, and listening
- Instant feedback on incorrect answers
- Remediation activities
- Robust assessments that include diagnostic tests, chapter review tests, mid- and end-of-term review tests, and final exams
- Gradebook and diagnostic tools that allow teachers to monitor student progress and analyze data to determine steps for remediation and support
- Student Book answer key in the Teacher Resource Folder

The Azar-Hagen Grammar Series consists of

- *Understanding and Using English Grammar* (blue cover), for upper-level students.
- *Fundamentals of English Grammar* (black), for mid-level students.
- *Basic English Grammar* (red), for lower or beginning levels.

Tips for Using the New Features in this Text

- **WARM-UPS**

The Warm-Up exercises are a brief pre-teaching tool for the charts. They highlight the key point(s) that will be introduced in the chart that follows the Warm-Up exercise. Before beginning the task, teachers will want to familiarize themselves with the material in the chart. Then, with the teacher's guidance, students can discover many or sometimes all of the new patterns as they complete the Warm-Up activity. After students finish the exercise, teachers may find that no further explanation is necessary, and the charts can serve as a useful reference.

- **LISTENING**

The Listening exercises have been designed to help students understand American English as it is actually spoken. As such, it includes reductions and other phenomena that are part of the natural, relaxed speech of everyday English. Because the audio uses English that may be spoken at a rate faster than what students are used to, they may need to hear sentences two or three times while completing a task.

The Listening exercises do not encourage immediate pronunciation (unless they are linked to a specific pronunciation task). Receptive skills precede productive ones, and it is essential that students be able to hear the speech patterns before they begin using them in their own speech.

Students are encouraged to listen to longer passages the first time through without looking at their text. Teachers can then explain any vocabulary that has not already been clarified. During the second listening, students complete the assigned task. Teachers will want to pause the audio appropriately. Depending on the level of the class, pauses may be needed after every sentence, or even within a sentence.

It is inevitable that sound representations in the text will at times differ from the instructor's speech, whether it be due to register or regional variation. As a general rule, if the instructor expects that students will hear a variation, or if students themselves raise the questions, alternate representations can be presented.

A listening script with all the listening exercises can be found at the back of the book.

- **READINGS**

The Readings give students an opportunity to work with the grammar structures in extended contexts. One approach is to have students read the passage alone the first time through. Then they work in small groups or as a class to clarify vocabulary questions. A second reading may be necessary. Varied reading tasks then allow students to check their comprehension, to use the target structures, and to expand upon the topic in speaking or writing.

- **WRITING TASKS**

As students gain confidence in using the target structures, they are encouraged to express their ideas in complete paragraphs. A model paragraph accompanies each assignment and question-prompts help students develop their ideas.

Peer editing can be used for correction. A useful technique is to pair students, have them exchange papers, and then have the *partner* read the paragraph aloud. The writer can *hear* if the content is what he or she intended. This also keeps the writer from automatically self-correcting while reading aloud. (Self-correcting can be a problem if writers are unaware that they are making corrections as they read.)

For classes that have not had much experience with writing, the teacher may want to assign students to small groups. Each group composes a paragraph together. The teacher collects the paragraph and adds comments, and then makes a copy for each group member. Students correct the paragraph *individually*.

When correcting student writing, teachers may want to focus primarily on the structures taught in the chapter.

• **LET'S TALK**

Each Let's Talk activity is set up as one of the following: **pairwork**, **small group**, **class activity**, **interview**, or **game**. Successful language learning requires social interaction, and these tasks encourage students to speak with others about their ideas, their everyday lives, and the world around them. Students tend to speak more easily and freely when they can connect language to their own knowledge and experiences.

• **CHECK YOUR KNOWLEDGE**

Toward the end of the chapter, students can practice sentence-level editing skills by correcting errors common to this level. The sentences can be done as homework or in small groups.

This task can easily be set up as a game. The teacher calls out an item number at random. Students work in teams to correct the sentence, and the first team to edit it correctly wins a point.

See the *Fundamentals of English Grammar Teacher's Guide* for detailed information about teaching from this book, including expansion activities and step-by-step instructions.

Acknowledgments

We couldn't have done this fourth edition without the many talented professionals who assisted us. We began our revision with the insights and suggestions from these reviewers: Michael Berman, Montgomery College; Jeff Bette, Westchester Community College; Mary Goodman, Everest University; Linda Gossard, DPT Business School, Denver; Roberta Hodges, Sonoma State American Language Institute; Suzanne Kelso, Boise State University; Steven Lasswell, Santa Barbara City College; Diane Mahin, University of Miami; Maria Mitchell, DPT Business School, Philadelphia; Monica Oliva, Miami Sunset Adult Center; Amy Parker, University of Michigan; Casey Peltier, Northern Virginia Community College.

We are fortunate to have an outstanding editorial staff who oversaw this book from planning to production. We'd like to thank Shelley Hartle, managing editor extraordinaire, whose meticulous and perceptive editing shaped every page; Amy McCormick, editorial director, whose vision, attentiveness, and care for the series guided our writing; Ruth Voetmann, development editor, for her keen eye, valuable advice, and unfailing patience; Janice Baillie, our outstanding copy-editor who scrutinized and honed every page; Sue Van Etten, our accomplished and very talented business and web-site manager; Robert Ruvo, our skilled and responsive production manager at Pearson Education.

We'd also like to express our appreciation to the writers of the supplementary texts: Rachel Spack Koch, *Workbook;* Kelly Roberts Weibel, *Test Bank;* and Martha Hall, *Teacher's Guide.* They have greatly enriched the series with their innovative ideas and creativity.

Finally, we'd like to thank the dedicated leadership team at Pearson Education that guided this project: Pietro Alongi, Rhea Banker, and Paula Van Ells.

The colorful artwork is due to the inspired talents of Don Martinetti and Chris Pavely.

Finally, we would like to thank our families, who supported and encouraged us every step of the way. They are a continual source of inspiration.

Betty S. Azar
Stacy A. Hagen

Chapter 8
Connecting Ideas

❑ **Exercise 1. Warm-up.** (Chart 8-1)
Check (✓) the sentences that have the correct punctuation.

1. _____ I ate an apple, and an orange.
2. _____ I ate an apple and an orange.
3. _____ I ate an apple, an orange, and a banana.
4. _____ I ate an apple, Nina ate a peach.
5. _____ I ate an apple, and Nina ate a peach.

8-1 Connecting Ideas with *And*

Connecting Items within a Sentence

(a) NO COMMA: I saw a cat *and* a mouse. (b) COMMAS: I saw a cat, a mouse, *and* a dog.	When *and* connects only TWO WORDS (or phrases) within a sentence, NO COMMA is used, as in (a). When *and* connects THREE OR MORE items within a sentence, COMMAS are used, as in (b).*

Connecting Two Sentences

(c) COMMA: I saw a cat, *and* you saw a mouse.	When *and* connects TWO COMPLETE SENTENCES (also called "independent" clauses), a COMMA is usually used, as in (c).
(d) PERIOD: I saw a cat. You saw a mouse. (e) *INCORRECT: I saw a cat, you saw a mouse.*	Without *and*, two complete sentences are separated by a period, as in (d), *not* a comma.** A complete sentence begins with a capital letter; note that *You* is capitalized in (d).

*In a series of three or more items, the comma before *and* is optional.
　　ALSO CORRECT: *I saw a cat, a mouse and a dog.*

**A "period" (the dot used at the end of a sentence) is called a "full stop" in British English.

❏ **Exercise 2. Looking at grammar.** (Chart 8-1)

<u>Underline</u> and label the words (noun, verb, adjective) connected by **and**. Add commas as necessary.

           noun + noun

1. My mom puts <u>milk</u> and <u>sugar</u> in her tea. → (*no commas needed*)

           noun + noun + noun

2. My mom puts <u>milk</u>, <u>sugar</u>, and <u>lemon</u> in her tea. → (*commas needed*)

3. The river is wide and deep.

4. The river is wide deep and dangerous.

5. The teenage girls at the slumber* party played music ate pizza and told ghost stories.

6. The teenage girls played music and ate pizza.

7. My mom dad sister and grandfather came to the party to see my son and daughter celebrate their fourth birthday.

8. When he wanted to entertain the children, my husband mooed like a cow roared like a lion and barked like a dog.

❏ **Exercise 3. Let's talk and write: interview.** (Chart 8-1)

Interview another student in your class. Take notes and then write complete sentences using **and**. Share some of the answers with the class.

What are . . .
1. your three favorite sports?
2. three adjectives that describe the weather today?
3. four cities that you would like to visit?
4. two characteristics that describe this city or town?
5. five things you did this morning?
6. three things you are afraid of?
7. two or more things that make you happy?
8. three or more adjectives that describe the people in your country?
9. the five most important qualities of a good parent?

---

*slumber = sleep; at a slumber party, friends sleep overnight together.

❑ **Exercise 4. Looking at grammar.** (Chart 8-1)
Add commas and periods where appropriate. Capitalize as necessary.

1. The rain fell. ^T̸he wind blew.

2. The rain fell, and the wind blew.*

3. I talked he listened.

4. I talked to Ryan about his school grades and he listened to me carefully.

5. The five most common words in English are *the and of to* and *a*.

6. The man asked a question the woman answered it.

7. The man asked a question and the woman answered it.

8. Rome is an Italian city it has a mild climate and many interesting attractions.

9. You should visit Rome its climate is mild and there are many interesting attractions.

❑ **Exercise 5. Warm-up.** (Chart 8-2)
Complete the sentences with your own ideas. Make true statements.

1. When I'm not sure of the meaning of a word in English, I _____

_____ or _____ .

2. Sometimes I don't understand native speakers of English, but I _____

_____ .

8-2 Connecting Ideas with *But* and *Or*

(a) I *went* to bed *but couldn't sleep*. (b) Is a lemon *sweet* **or** *sour*? (c) Did you order *coffee, tea,* **or** *milk*?	***And, but,*** and ***or*** are called "coordinating conjunctions." Like ***and, but*** and ***or*** can connect items within a sentence. Commas are used with a series of three or more items, as in (c).
I dropped the vase. = a sentence *It didn't break.* = a sentence (d) I dropped the vase, ***but*** it didn't break. (e) Do we have class on Monday, ***or*** is Monday a holiday?	A comma is usually used when ***but*** or ***or*** combines two complete (independent) sentences into one sentence, as in (d) and (e). A conjunction can also come at the beginning of a sentence, except in formal writing. ALSO CORRECT: I dropped the vase. But it didn't break. I saw a cat. And you saw a mouse.

---

*Sometimes the comma is omitted when ***and*** connects two very short independent clauses.
ALSO CORRECT: *The rain fell ***and*** the wind blew.* (NO COMMA)
In longer sentences, the comma is helpful and usual.

□ **Exercise 6. Looking at grammar.** (Charts 8-1 and 8-2)
Complete the sentences with **and**, **but**, or **or**. Add commas as necessary.

1. I washed my shirt, _*but*_ it didn't get clean.

2. Would you like some water _*or*_ some fruit juice?

3. I bought some paper, a birthday card, _*and*_ some envelopes.

4. The flight attendants served dinner _____ I didn't eat it.

5. I was hungry _____ didn't eat on the plane. The food didn't look appetizing.

6. I washed my face, brushed my teeth _____ combed my hair.

7. Golf _____ tennis are popular sports.

8. Sara is a good tennis player _____ she's never played golf.

9. Which would you prefer? Would you like to play tennis _____ golf Saturday?

10. Who made the call? Did Bob call you _____ did you call Bob?

□ **Exercise 7. Looking at grammar.** (Charts 8-1 and 8-2)
Add commas, periods, and capital letters as necessary.

Electronic devices* on airplanes

1. Laptops are electronic devices. *C*ell phones are electronic devices.

2. Laptops and portable DVD players are electronic devices but flashlights aren't.

3. Passengers can't use these electronic devices during takeoffs and landings they can use them the rest of the flight.

4. During takeoffs and landings, airlines don't allow passengers to use laptops DVD players electronic readers or PDAs.**

5. The devices may cause problems with the navigation system and they may cause problems with the communication system.

□ **Exercise 8. Warm-up.** (Chart 8-3)
Match the sentences in Column A with a logical idea from Column B.

Column A
1. I was tired, so I _____ .
2. I was tired, but I _____ .

Column B
a. didn't sleep
b. slept

---

*device = a thing, often electric or electronic, that has a specific purpose

**PDA = personal digital assistant; a small device that has some computer functions

8-3 Connecting Ideas with *So*

(a) The room was dark, **so** I turned on a light.	**So** can be used as a conjunction, as in (a). It is preceded by a comma. It connects the ideas in two independent clauses.

	So expresses **results**:
	    cause: *The room was dark.*
	    result: *I turned on a light.*

(b) COMPARE: The room was dark, **but** I didn't turn on a light.	**But** often expresses an unexpected result, as in (b).

❑ **Exercise 9. Looking at grammar.** (Charts 8-2 and 8-3)
Complete the sentences with **so** or **but**.

1. It began to rain, ___so___ I opened my umbrella.

2. It began to rain, ___but___ I didn't open my umbrella.

3. I didn't have an umbrella, _____ I got wet.

4. I didn't have an umbrella, _____ I didn't get wet because I was wearing my raincoat.

5. The water was cold, _____ I went swimming anyway.

6. The water was cold, _____ I didn't go swimming.

7. Scott's directions to his apartment weren't clear, _____ Sonia got lost.

8. The directions weren't clear, _____ I found Scott's apartment anyway.

9. My friend lied to me, _____ I still like and trust her.

10. My friend lied to me, _____ I don't trust her anymore.

❑ **Exercise 10. Looking at grammar.** (Charts 8-1 → 8-3)
Add commas, periods, and capital letters as necessary.

Surprising animal facts:

1. Some tarantulas* can go two and a half years without food. When they eat, they like grasshoppers beetles small spiders and sometimes small lizards.

2. A female elephant is pregnant for approximately twenty months and almost always has only one baby a young elephant stays close to its mother for the first ten years of its life.

---

tarantula = a big, hairy spider

3. Dolphins sleep with one eye open they need to be conscious or awake in order to breathe if they fall asleep when they are breathing, they will drown so they sleep with half their brain awake and one eye open.

❑ **Exercise 11. Listening and grammar.** (Charts 8-1 → 8-3)
Listen to the passage. Then add commas, periods, and capital letters as necessary. Listen again as you check your answers. Before you begin, you may want to check your understanding of these words: *blinker, do a good deed, motioned, wave someone on.*

Paying It Forward*

(1)   *A* a few days ago, a friend and I were driving from Benton Harbor to Chicago.

(2)   *W* we didn't have any delays for the first hour but we ran into some highway construction

(3)   near Chicago the traffic wasn't moving my friend and I sat and waited we talked about

(4)   our jobs our families and the terrible traffic slowly it started to move

(5)   we noticed a black sports car on the shoulder its blinker was on the driver

(6)   obviously wanted to get back into traffic car after car passed without letting him in I

(7)   decided to do a good deed so I motioned for him to get in line ahead of me he waved

(8)   thanks and I waved back at him

(9)   all the cars had to stop at a toll booth a short way down the road I held out my

(10) money to pay my toll but the toll-taker just smiled and waved me on she told me that the

(11) man in the black sports car had already paid my toll wasn't that a nice way of saying

(12) thank you?

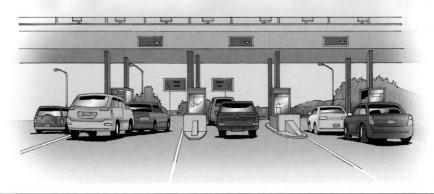

---

*paying it forward = doing something nice for someone after someone does something nice for you. For example, imagine you are at a coffee stand waiting to buy a cup of coffee. The person in front of you is chatting with you and pays for your cup of coffee. You then buy a cup of coffee for the next person in line. You are *paying it forward*.

Paying it forward means the opposite of *paying it back* (repaying a debt or an obligation).

Exercise 12. Warm-up. (Chart 8-4)
Complete the sentences. Make true statements.

1. I like _____fish_____, but ___my sister___ doesn't.

2. I don't like _____, but _____ does.

3. I've seen _____, but _____ hasn't.

4. I'm not _____, but _____ is.

8-4 Using Auxiliary Verbs after *But*

(a) I **don't like** coffee, **but** my husband **does**.	After **but**, often only an auxiliary verb is used. It has the same tense or modal as the main verb.
(b) I **like** tea, **but** my husband **doesn't**.	In (a): **does** = likes coffee
(c) I **won't be** here tomorrow, **but** Sue **will**.	Notice in the examples:
(d) I**'ve seen** that movie, **but** Joe **hasn't**.	negative + **but** + affirmative
(e) He **isn't** here, **but** she **is**.*	affirmative + **but** + negative

*A verb is not contracted with a pronoun at the end of a sentence after **but** and **and**:
    CORRECT: . . . but she is.
    INCORRECT: . . . but she's.

□ **Exercise 13. Looking at grammar.** (Chart 8-4)
Part I. Complete each sentence with the correct negative auxiliary verb.

1. Alan reads a lot of books, but his brother ___doesn't___.

2. Alan reads a lot of books, but his brothers ___don't___.

3. Alan is reading a book, but his brother _____.

4. Alan is reading a book, but his brothers _____.

5. Alan read a book last week, but his brother(s) _____.

6. Alan has read a book recently, but his brother _____.

7. Alan has read a book recently, but his brothers _____.

8. Alan is going to read a book soon, but his brother _____.

9. Alan is going to read a book soon, but his brothers _____.

10. Alan will read a book soon, but his brother(s) _____.

Part II. Complete each sentence with the correct affirmative auxiliary verb.

1. Nicole doesn't eat red meat, but her sister ___does___.

2. Nicole doesn't eat red meat, but her sisters ___do___.

3. Nicole isn't eating red meat, but her sister _____.

4. Nicole isn't eating red meat, but her sisters _____.

5. Nicole didn't eat red meat last night, but her sister(s) _____.

6. Nicole hasn't eaten red meat recently, but her sister _____.

7. Nicole hasn't eaten red meat recently, but her sisters _____.

8. Nicole isn't going to eat red meat soon, but her sister _____.

9. Nicole isn't going to eat red meat soon, but her sisters _____.

10. Nicole won't eat red meat soon, but her sister(s) _____.

❑ **Exercise 14. Let's talk.** (Chart 8-4)
Complete the sentences with true statements about your classmates. You may need to interview them to get more information. Use appropriate auxiliary verbs.

1. ___*Kira*___ has long hair, but ___*Yuki doesn't*_____.

2. _____ isn't hungry right now, but _____.

3. _____ lives nearby, but _____.

4. _____ can speak (*a language*) _____, but _____.

5. _____ plays a musical instrument, but _____.

6. _____ wasn't here last year, but _____.

7. _____ will be at home tonight, but _____.

8. _____ doesn't wear a ring, but _____.

9. _____ didn't study here last year, but _____.

10. _____ has lived here for a long time, but _____.

❑ **Exercise 15. Listening.** (Chart 8-4)
Complete the sentences with appropriate auxiliary verbs.

A strong storm

Example: You will hear: My husband saw a tree fall, but I . . .
You will write: ___*didn't*___ .

1. _____ .   5. _____ .

2. _____ .   6. _____ .

3. _____ .   7. _____ .

4. _____ .   8. _____ .

❑ **Exercise 16. Warm-up.** (Chart 8-5)
Match each sentence with the correct picture. NOTE: One picture doesn't match any of the sentences.

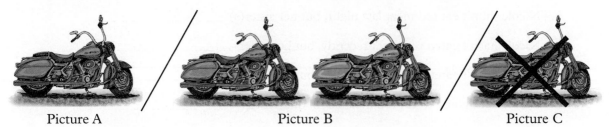

Picture A   Picture B   Picture C

1. _____ Alice has a motorcycle, and her husband does too.

2. _____ Alice has a motorcycle, and so does her husband.

3. _____ Alice doesn't have a motorcycle, and her husband doesn't either.

4. _____ Alice doesn't have a motorcycle, and neither does her husband.

8-5 Using *And* + *Too, So, Either, Neither*

S + AUX + *TOO*
(a) Sue works, *and* **Tom does too.**
 	
SO + AUX + S
(b) Sue works, *and* **so   does Tom.**
	In affirmative statements, an auxiliary verb + **too** or **so** can be used after **and**.
	
	Examples (a) and (b) have the same meaning.
	
	Word order:
	    subject + *auxiliary* + **too**
	    so + *auxiliary* + *subject*

S + AUX   + *EITHER*
(c) Ann doesn't work, *and* **Joe doesn't   either.**
 	
NEITHER + AUX + S
(d) Ann doesn't work, *and* **neither   does Joe.**
	An auxiliary verb + **either** or **neither** are used with negative statements.
	Examples (c) and (d) have the same meaning.
	Word order:
	    subject + *auxiliary* + **either**
	    neither + *auxiliary* + *subject*
	
	NOTE: An affirmative auxiliary is used with *neither*.

(e) — I'm hungry.
    — *I am too. / So am I.*
 	
(f) — I don't eat meat.
    — *I don't either. / Neither do I.*
	And is not usually used when there are two speakers.

(g) — I'm hungry.
    — *Me too.* (*informal*)
 	
(h) — I don't eat meat.
    — *Me* (*n*)*either.* (*informal*)
	Me too, **me either**, and **me neither** are often used in informal spoken English.

Exercise 17. Looking at grammar. (Chart 8-5)
Complete the sentences with the given words. Pay special attention to word order.

       Omar   James   Marco   Ivan

1. a. too   Marco has a mustache, and __*James does too*_____.

    b. so   Marco has a mustache, and _____.

2. a. either Omar doesn't have a mustache, and _____.

    b. neither Omar doesn't have a mustache, and _____.

3. a. too   Marco is wearing a hat, and _____.

    b. so   Marco is wearing a hat, and _____.

4. a. either Ivan isn't wearing a hat, and _____.

    b. neither Ivan isn't wearing a hat, and _____.

Exercise 18. Looking at grammar. (Chart 8-5)
Part I. Complete each sentence with the correct affirmative auxiliary verb.

1. Andy walks to work, and his roommate __*does*__ too.

2. Andy walks to work, and his roommates _____ too.

3. Andy is walking to work, and his roommate _____ too.

4. Andy is walking to work, and his roommates _____ too.

5. Andy walked to work last week, and his roommate(s) _____ too.

6. Andy has walked to work recently, and so _____ his roommate.

7. Andy has walked to work recently, and so _____ his roommates.

8. Andy is going to walk to work tomorrow, and so _____ his roommate.

9. Andy is going to walk to work tomorrow, and so _____ his roommates.

10. Andy will walk to work tomorrow, and so _____ his roommate(s).

Part II. Complete each sentence with the correct negative auxiliary verb.

1. Karen doesn't watch TV, and her sister ___doesn't___ either.

2. Karen doesn't watch TV, and her sisters _____ either.

3. Karen isn't watching TV, and her sister _____ either.

4. Karen isn't watching TV, and her sisters _____ either

5. Karen didn't watch TV last night, and her sister(s) _____ either.

6. Karen hasn't watched TV recently, and neither _____ her sister.

7. Karen hasn't watched TV recently, and neither _____ her sisters.

8. Karen isn't going to watch TV tomorrow, neither _____ her sister.

9. Karen isn't going to watch TV tomorrow, and neither _____ her sisters.

10. Karen won't watch TV tomorrow, and neither _____ her sister(s).

□ **Exercise 19. Let's talk and write.** (Chart 8-5)
Work in small groups. Complete the sentences with *too, so, either,* or *neither.* Make true statements. You may need to research your answers.

1. Haiti is a small country, and ___Cuba is too_____.

2. Japan produces rice, and _____.

3. Turkey has had many strong earthquakes, and _____.

4. Iceland doesn't grow coffee, and _____.

5. Most Canadian children will learn more than one language, and _____

   _____.

6. Norway joined the United Nations in 1945, and _____.

7. Argentina doesn't lie on the equator, and _____.

8. Somalia lies on the Indian Ocean, and _____.

9. Monaco has never* hosted the Olympic Games, and _____.

10. South Korea had a Nobel Prize winner in 2000, and _____.

Never makes a sentence negative: *The teacher is **never** late, and **neither** am I.* OR *I'm **not either**.*

☐ **Exercise 20. Let's talk: pairwork.** (Chart 8-5)
Work with a partner. Speaker A says the given sentence. Speaker B agrees with Speaker A's
statement by using *so* or *neither*.

Example: I'm confused.
SPEAKER A (*book open*): I'm confused.
SPEAKER B (*book closed*): So am I.

1. I studied last night.
2. I study grammar every day.
3. I'd like a cup of coffee.
4. I'm not hungry.
5. I've never seen a vampire.
6. Running is an aerobic activity.
7. Snakes don't have legs.
8. Coffee contains caffeine.

Change roles.
9. I overslept this morning.
10. I don't like mushrooms.
11. Swimming is an Olympic sport.
12. Denmark doesn't have any volcanoes.
13. I've never touched a crocodile.
14. Chickens lay eggs.
15. Elephants can swim.
16. I'd rather go to (*name of a place*) than (*name of a place*).

☐ **Exercise 21. Let's listen and talk.** (Chart 8-5)
There are responses you can use if you don't agree with someone else's statement.

Part I. Listen to the examples. As you listen, pay special attention to the sentence stress in
items 4–6 when Speaker B is disagreeing.

To get more information:
1. A: I'm going to drop this class.
   B: **You are? Why? What's the matter?**

2. A: My laptop doesn't have enough memory for this application.
   B: **Really? Are you sure?**

3. A: I can read Braille.
   B: **You can? How did you learn to do that?**

To disagree:
4. A: I love this weather.
   B: **I don't.**

5. A: I didn't like the movie.
   B: **I did!**

6. A: I'm excited about graduation.
   B: **I'm not.**

Part II. Work with a partner. Partner A will make a statement, and Partner B will ask for more information. Take turns saying the sentences.

1. I'm feeling tired.
2. I don't like grammar.
3. I've seen a ghost.
4. I didn't eat breakfast this morning.
5. I haven't slept well all week.
6. I'm going to leave class early.

Part III. Now take turns disagreeing with the given statements.

7. I believe in ghosts.
8. I didn't study hard for the last test.
9. I'm going to exercise for an hour today.
10. I like strawberries.
11. I haven't worked very hard this week.
12. I don't enjoy birthdays.

❑ **Exercise 22. Let's talk.** (Charts 8-4 and 8-5)
Make true statements about your classmates using *and* and *but*. You may need to interview them to get more information. Use the appropriate auxiliary verbs.

1. ___*Kunio*___ lives in an apartment, and ___*Boris does too*___ .

2. ___*Ellen*___ is wearing jeans, but ___*Ricardo isn't*___ .

3. _____ is absent today, but _____ .

4. _____ didn't live here last year, and _____ either.

5. _____ can cook, and _____ too.

6. _____ has a baseball cap, and _____ too.

7. _____ doesn't have a motorcycle, and _____ either.

8. _____ doesn't have a pet, but _____ .

9. _____ will get up early tomorrow, but _____ .

10. _____ has studied English for more than a year, and _____ too.

❑ **Exercise 23. Warm-up.** (Chart 8-6)
Circle all the logical completions.

Because Roger felt tired, _____ .

   a. he took a nap.   c. he went to bed early.
   b. he didn't take a nap.   d. he didn't go to bed early.

8-6 Connecting Ideas with *Because*

(a) He drank water **because** he was thirsty.	**Because** expresses a cause; it gives a reason. Why did he drink water? *Reason:* He was thirsty.
(b) MAIN CLAUSE: *He drank water.*	A main clause is a complete sentence: **He drank water** = a complete sentence
(c) ADVERB CLAUSE: *because he was thirsty*	An adverb clause is NOT a complete sentence: **because he was thirsty** = NOT a complete sentence **Because** introduces an adverb clause: **because** + *subject* + *verb* = *an adverb clause*

MAIN CLAUSE   ADVERB CLAUSE
(d) He drank water **because** he was thirsty.
     (no comma)
 	
   ADVERB CLAUSE   MAIN CLAUSE
(e) **Because** he was thirsty, he drank water.
     (comma)
	An adverb clause is connected to a main clause, as in (d) and (e).
	In (d): *main clause + no comma + adverb clause*
	In (e): *adverb clause + comma + main clause*
	Examples (d) and (e) have exactly the same meaning.

(f) INCORRECT IN WRITING: He drank water. *Because he was thirsty.*	Example (f) is incorrect in written English: **Because he was thirsty** cannot stand alone as a sentence that starts with a capital letter and ends with a period. It has to be connected to a main clause, as in (d) and (e).
(g) CORRECT IN SPEAKING: — Why did he drink some water? — **Because he was thirsty.**	In spoken English, an adverb clause can be used as the short answer to a question, as in (g).

❏ **Exercise 24. Looking at grammar.** (Chart 8-6)
Combine each pair of sentences in two different orders. Use *because*. Punctuate carefully.

1. We didn't have class. \ The teacher was absent.
   → *We didn't have class because the teacher was absent.*
   → *Because the teacher was absent, we didn't have class.*

2. The children were hungry. \ There was no food in the house.

3. The bridge is closed. \ We can't get across the river.

4. My car didn't start. \ The battery was dead.

5. Talya and Patti laughed hard. \ The joke was very funny.

❏ **Exercise 25. Looking at grammar.** (Chart 8-6)
Add periods, commas, and capital letters as necessary.

1. Jimmy is very young. ~~b~~ᴮecause he is afraid of the dark, he likes to have a light on in his bedroom at night.

2. Mr. El-Sayed had a bad cold because he was not feeling well he stayed home from the office.

3. Judy went to bed early because she was tired she likes to get at least eight hours of sleep a night.

4. Frank put his head in his hands he was angry and upset because he had lost a lot of work on his computer.

☐ **Exercise 26. Looking at grammar.** (Charts 8-3 and 8-6)
Make sentences with the same meaning as the given sentence. Use commas where appropriate.

Part I. Restate the sentences. Use ***so***.

1. Wendy lost her job because she never showed up for work on time.

    → *Wendy never showed up for work on time*, so she lost her job.

2. I opened the window because the room was hot.

3. Because it was raining, I stayed indoors.

Part II. Restate the sentences. Use ***because***.

4. Jason was hungry, so he ate.

    → *Because Jason was hungry*, he ate. OR *Jason ate because he was hungry.*

5. The water in the river is polluted, so we shouldn't go swimming there.

6. My alarm clock didn't go off,★ so I was late for my job interview.

☐ **Exercise 27. Looking at grammar.** (Charts 8-1 → 8-6)
Add commas, periods, and capital letters where appropriate. Don't change any of the words or the order of the words.

1. Jim was hot. *H*he sat in the shade.

2. Jim was hot and tired so he sat in the shade.

3. Jim was hot tired and thirsty.

4. Because he was hot Jim sat in the shade.

5. Because they were hot and thirsty Jim and Susan sat in the shade and drank iced-tea.

6. Jim and Susan sat in the shade and drank iced-tea because they were hot and thirsty.

7. Jim sat in the shade drank iced-tea and fanned himself with his cap because he was hot tired and thirsty.

8. Because Jim was hot he stayed under the shade of the tree but Susan went back to work.

★*go off* = ring

□ **Exercise 28. Listening.** (Charts 8-1 → 8-6)
Listen to the passage. Then add commas, periods, and capital letters where appropriate. Listen again as you check your answers.

Understanding the Scientific Term *Matter*

The word *matter* is a chemical term. $\overset{M}{\cancel{m}}$atter is anything that has weight this book your

finger water a rock air and the moon are all examples of matter heat and radio waves are not matter

because they do not have weight happiness dreams and fears have no weight and are not matter.

□ **Exercise 29. Warm-up.** (Chart 8-7)
In which sentences is the result (in green) the opposite of what you expect?

1. Even though I didn't eat dinner last night, I wasn't hungry this morning.
2. Because I didn't eat dinner last night, I was hungry this morning.
3. Although I didn't eat dinner last night, I wasn't hungry this morning.

8-7	Connecting Ideas with *Even Though/Although*	
(a)	**Even though** I was hungry, I did not eat. I did not eat **even though** I was hungry.	**Even though** and **although** introduce an adverb clause.
(b)	**Although** I was hungry, I did not eat. I did not eat **although** I was hungry.	Examples (a) and (b) have the same meaning: *I was hungry, but I did not eat.*
	COMPARE: (c) **Because** I was hungry, *I ate.* (d) **Even though** I was hungry, *I did not eat.*	**Because** expresses an expected result, as in (c). **Even though/although** expresses an unexpected or opposite result, as in (d).

□ **Exercise 30. Looking at grammar.** (Chart 8-7)
Complete the sentences with the given words.

1. *is, isn't*

   a. Because Dan is sick, he _____ going to work.

   b. Although Dan is sick, he _____ going to work.

   c. Even though Dan is sick, he _____ going to work.

2. *went, didn't go*

   a. Even though it was late, we _____ home.

   b. Although it was late, we _____ home.

   c. Because it was late, we _____ home.

❏ **Exercise 31. Looking at grammar.** (Chart 8-7)
Complete the sentences with *even though* or *because*.

1. <u>   Even though   </u> the weather is cold, Rick isn't wearing a coat.

2. <u>   Because   </u> the weather is cold, Ben is wearing a coat.

3. _____ Jane was sad, she smiled.

4. _____ Jane was sad, she cried.

5. _____ it was cold outside, we went swimming in the lake.

6. _____ our friends live on an island, it isn't easy to get there by car.

7. People ask Kelly to sing at weddings _____ she has a good voice.

8. _____ I'm training for the Olympics, I biked up the mountain
_____ it was starting to snow.

9. George sings loudly _____ he can't carry a tune.

❏ **Exercise 32. Looking at grammar.** (Charts 8-6 and 8-7)
Choose the best completion for each sentence.

1. Even though the test was fairly easy, most of the class _____ .
   a. failed
   b. passed
   c. did pretty well

2. Jack hadn't heard or read about the bank robbery even though _____ .
   a. he was the robber
   b. it was on the front page of every newspaper
   c. he was out of town when it occurred

3. Although _____ , she finished the race in first place.
   a. Miki was full of energy and strength
   b. Miki was leading all the way
   c. Miki was far behind in the beginning

4. We can see the light from an airplane at night before we can hear the plane because _____ .
   a. light travels faster than sound
   b. airplanes travel at high speeds
   c. our eyes work better than our ears at night

5. My partner and I worked all day and late into the evening. Even though _____ , we stopped at our favorite restaurant before we went home.
   a. we were very hungry
   b. we had finished our report
   c. we were very tired

6. In the mountains, melting snow in the spring runs downhill into rivers. The water carries soil and rocks. In the spring, mountain rivers become muddy rather than clear because _____ .
   a. mountain tops are covered with snow
   b. the water from melting snow brings soil and rocks to the river
   c. ice is frozen water

☐ **Exercise 33. Listening.** (Charts 8-6 and 8-7)
Choose the best completion for each sentence.

Example: You will hear: Because there was a sale at the mall, . . .
You will choose: a. it wasn't busy.
                  (b.) there were a lot of shoppers.
                   c. prices were very high.

1. a. they were under some mail.
   b. my roommate helped me look for them.
   c. I never found them.

2. a. the rain had stopped.
   b. a storm was coming.
   c. the weather was nice.

3. a. he was sick.
   b. he had graduated already.
   c. he was happy for me.

4. a. I mailed it.
   b. I decided not to mail it.
   c. I sent it to a friend.

5. a. the coaches celebrated afterwards.
   b. the fans cheered loudly.
   c. the players didn't seem very excited.

❑ **Exercise 34. Let's talk.** (Charts 8-6 and 8-7)
Answer the questions in complete sentences, using either **because** or **even though**. Work in pairs, in small groups, or as a class.

Example: Last night you were tired. Did you go to bed early?
→ *Yes, I went to bed early because I was tired.* OR
→ *Yes, because I was tired, I went to bed before nine.* OR
→ *No, I didn't go to bed early even though I was really sleepy.* OR
→ *No, even though I was really tired, I didn't go to bed until after midnight.*

1. Last night you were tired. Did you stay up late?
2. Vegetables are good for you. Do you eat a lot of them?
3. Space exploration is exciting. Would you like to be an astronaut?
4. What are the winters like here? Do you like living here in the winter?
5. (*A recent movie*) has had good reviews. Do you want to see it?
6. Are you a good artist? Will you draw a picture of me on the board?
7. Where does your family live? Are you going to visit them over the next holiday?

❑ **Exercise 35. Reading and grammar.** (Chapter 8)
Part I. Read the passage.

The Importance of Water

What is the most common substance on earth? It isn't wood, iron, or sand. The most common substance on earth is water. Every living thing contains water. For example, a person's body is about 67 percent water, a bird's is about 75 percent water, and most fruit contains about 90 percent water.

In addition, 70 percent of the earth's surface is water. Besides being in lakes, rivers, and oceans, water is in the ground and in the air. However, most of the water in the world is saltwater. Only 3 percent of the earth's water is fresh, and just one percent of that is available for human use. The rest is saltwater, and people can't drink it or grow food with it.

Water is essential to life, but human beings often poison it with chemicals from industry and farming. When people pollute water, the quality of all life — plant life, animal life, and human life — suffers. Life cannot exist without fresh water, so it is essential that people take care of this important natural resource.

Part II. Complete the sentences with **because/although/even though/so**.

1. _____ 70 percent of the earth's surface is water and water is in every living thing, it is the most common substance on earth.

2. _____ 70 percent of the earth's surface is water, only 3 percent is fresh.

3. _____ water is everywhere, not much is available for human use.

4. Chemicals pollute water, _____ it is important to keep them out of the water supply.

5. _____ water is essential to human life, people need to take care of it.

6. Water is essential to human life, _____ people need to take care of it.

❑ **Exercise 36. Check your knowledge.** (Chapter 8)
Edit the sentences. Correct the errors in sentence structure. Pay special attention to punctuation.

1. Even though I was sick, ~~but~~ I went to work.

2. Gold silver and copper. They are metals.

3. The children crowded around the teacher. Because he was doing a magic trick.

4. I had a cup of coffee, and so does my friend.

5. My roommate didn't go. Neither I went either.

6. Even I was exhausted, I didn't stop working until after midnight.

7. Although I like chocolate, but I can't eat it because I'm allergic to it.

8. I like to eat raw eggs for breakfast and everybody else in my family too.

9. A hardware store sells tools and nails and plumbing supplies and paint.

10. Most insects have wings, spiders do not.

❑ **Exercise 37. Let's write.** (Chapter 8)
Write about an animal that interests you. Follow these steps:

1. Choose an animal you want to know more about.

   Hint: If you are doing your research on the Internet, type in "interesting facts about _____ ."

2. Take notes on the information you find. For example, here is some information about giraffes from an Internet site.

   Sample notes:

   Giraffes
   → have long necks (6 feet or 1.8 meters)
   → can reach tops of trees
   → need very little sleep (20 minutes to two hours out of 24 hours)
   → eat about 140 pounds of food a day
   → can go for weeks without drinking water
   → get a lot of water from the plants they eat
   → can grab and hold onto objects with their tongues
   → don't have vocal cords
   → can communicate with one another
      (but humans can't hear them)

3. Write sentences based on your facts. Combine some of the ideas using **and, but, or, so, because, although, even though**.

Sample sentences:

Giraffes
→ Giraffes have long necks, so they can reach the tops of trees.
→ Although they eat about 140 pounds of food a day, they can go for weeks without drinking water.
→ Even though giraffes don't have vocal cords, they can communicate with one another.
→ Giraffes can communicate, but people can't hear their communication.

4. Put your sentences into a paragraph.

Sample paragraph:

Interesting Facts About Giraffes

Giraffes are interesting animals. They have long necks, so they can reach the tops of trees. They eat flowers, fruit, climbing plants, and the twigs and leaves from trees. Although they eat about 140 pounds of food a day, they can go for weeks without drinking water. They get a lot of water from the plants they eat too. They have very long tongues and these tongues are useful. Because they are so long, they can grab objects with them. Even though giraffes don't have vocal cords, they can communicate, but people can't hear their communication.

Chapter 9
Comparisons

❑ **Exercise 1. Warm-up.** (Chart 9-1)
Compare the lengths of the lines.

1. Line D is as long as Line _____ .
2. Line A isn't as long as Line _____ .
3. Line E is almost as long as Line _____ .

Line A _____
Line B _____
Line C _____
Line D _____
Line E _____

9-1 Making Comparisons with *As . . . As*

(a) Tina is 21 years old. Sam is also 21. Tina is *as old as* Sam (is).	*As . . . as* is used to say that the two parts of a comparison are equal or the same in some way. In (a): *as + adjective + as*
(b) Mike came *as quickly as* he could.	In (b): *as + adverb + as*
(c) Ted is 20. Tina is 21. Ted is *not as old as* Tina. (d) Ted is *not quite as old as* Tina. (e) Amy is 5. She is *not nearly as old as* Tina.	Negative form: *not as . . . as.** *Quite* and *nearly* are often used with the negative. In (d): *not quite as . . . as* = a small difference. In (e): *not nearly as . . . as* = a big difference.
(f) Sam is *just as old as* Tina. (g) Ted is *nearly/almost as old as* Tina.	Common modifiers of *as . . . as* are *just* (meaning "exactly") and *nearly/almost.*

Tina	Sam	Ted	Amy
21	21	20	5

*Also possible: *not so . . . as: Ted is **not so** old as Tina.*

☐ **Exercise 2. Looking at grammar.** (Chart 9-1)
Complete the sentences, with *just as*, *almost as/not quite as*, or *not nearly as*.

Part I. Compare the fullness of the glasses.

1. Glass 4 is _____almost as / not quite as_____ full as Glass 2.

2. Glass 3 is _____ full as Glass 2.

3. Glass 1 is _____ full as Glass 2.

Part II. Compare the size of the boxes.

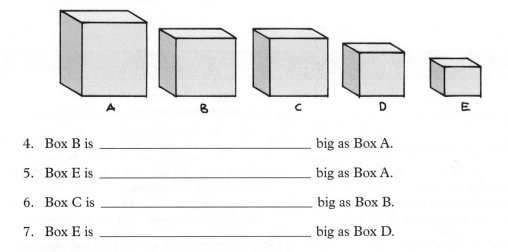

4. Box B is _____ big as Box A.

5. Box E is _____ big as Box A.

6. Box C is _____ big as Box B.

7. Box E is _____ big as Box D.

☐ **Exercise 3. Looking at grammar.** (Chart 9-1)
Complete the sentences with *as . . . as* and words from the list. Give your own opinion.
Use negative verbs where appropriate.

a housefly / an ant	good health / money
a lake / an ocean	honey / sugar
a lemon / a watermelon	monkeys /people
a lion / a tiger	reading a book / listening to music
a shower / a bath	the sun / the moon

1. _An ant isn't as_ _____ big as ___a housefly_____ .

2. _A lion is as_ _____ dangerous and wild as ___a tiger_____ .

3. _____ large as _____ .

4. _____ sweet as _____ .

5. _____ important as _____ .

6. _____ quiet as _____ .

7. _____ hot as _____ .

8. _____ good at climbing trees as _____ .

9. _____ relaxing as _____ .

☐ **Exercise 4. Listening.** (Chart 9-1)

Complete the sentences with the words you hear.

Sylvia   Brigita   Lara   Tanya
30   28   50   50

Example: You will hear: Brigita isn't as old as Lara.

You will write: ___isn't as old as___

1. Lara _____ Tanya.

2. Sylvia _____ Lara.

3. Sylvia and Brigita _____ Tanya.

4. Brigita _____ Sylvia.

5. Brigita _____ Sylvia.

❏ **Exercise 5. Game.** (Chart 9-1)

As . . . as is used in many traditional phrases. These phrases are generally spoken rather than written. See how many of them you're familiar with by completing the sentences with the given words. Work in teams. The team with the most correct answers wins.

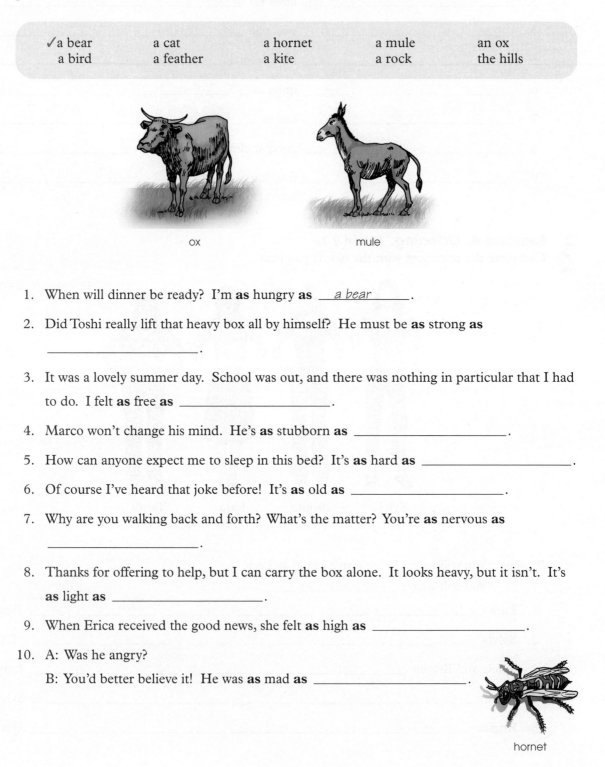

✓a bear	a cat	a hornet	a mule	an ox
a bird	a feather	a kite	a rock	the hills

ox

mule

1. When will dinner be ready? I'm **as** hungry **as** _____*a bear*_____.

2. Did Toshi really lift that heavy box all by himself? He must be **as** strong **as**

   _____.

3. It was a lovely summer day. School was out, and there was nothing in particular that I had to do. I felt **as** free **as** _____.

4. Marco won't change his mind. He's **as** stubborn **as** _____.

5. How can anyone expect me to sleep in this bed? It's **as** hard **as** _____.

6. Of course I've heard that joke before! It's **as** old **as** _____.

7. Why are you walking back and forth? What's the matter? You're **as** nervous **as**

   _____.

8. Thanks for offering to help, but I can carry the box alone. It looks heavy, but it isn't. It's **as** light **as** _____.

9. When Erica received the good news, she felt **as** high **as** _____.

10. A: Was he angry?

    B: You'd better believe it! He was **as** mad **as** _____.

hornet

❑ **Exercise 6. Warm-up.** (Chart 9-2)
Compare the people.

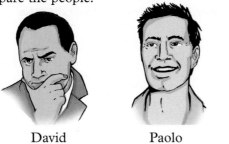

David   Paolo   Matt

    1. Paolo looks younger than _____.

    2. Matt looks younger than _____.

    3. _____ looks the youngest of all.

9-2 Comparative and Superlative

(a) "A" is *older than* "B."	The comparative compares *this* to *that* or *these* to *those*.
(b) "A" and "B" are *older than* "C" and "D."	Form: *-er* or *more* (See Chart 9-3.)
(c) Ed is *more generous than* his brother.	Notice: A comparative is followed by *than*.
(d) "A," "B," "C," and "D" are sisters. "A" is *the oldest of all* four sisters.	The superlative compares one part of a whole group to all the rest of the group.
(e) A woman in Turkey claims to be *the oldest person* in the world.	Form: *-est* or *most* (See Chart 9-3 for forms.)
(f) Ed is *the most generous person* in his family.	Notice: A superlative begins with *the*.

❑ **Exercise 7. Game.** (Chart 9-2)
Work in teams. Decide if the sentences are true (T) or false (F). The team with the most correct answers wins.

		T	F
1.	Canada is larger than France.	T	F
2.	Russia and Canada are the largest countries in the world.	T	F
3.	The South Pole is generally colder than the North Pole.	T	F
4.	The Pacific Ocean is the coldest ocean in the world.	T	F
5.	The Mediterranean Sea is the biggest sea of all.	T	F
6.	In general, Libya is hotter than Mexico.	T	F
7.	Africa is larger than Asia.	T	F
8.	Argentina has the highest and lowest points in South America.	T	F
9.	The nearest continent to Antarctica is Australia.	T	F
10.	The longest country in the world is Chile.	T	F

□ **Exercise 8. Listening.** (Charts 9-1 and 9-2)

Listen to the statements. Do you agree or disagree? Circle *yes* or *no*. Before you begin, you may want to check your understanding of these words: *talkative, cooked, tasty, raw.*

1. yes   no

2. yes   no

3. yes   no

4. yes   no

5. yes   no

6. yes   no

7. yes   no

8. yes   no

□ **Exercise 9. Warm-up.** (Chart 9-3)

Compare the three handwriting samples.

A: *The meeting starts at eight!*

B: *The meeting starts at eight*

C: *The meeting starts at eight!*

1. __C__ is neater than __A (or B)__ .

2. _____ is messier than _____.

3. _____ is more readable than _____.

4. _____ is better than _____.

5. _____ is the best.

6. _____ is the worst.

7. _____ wrote more carefully than _____.

9-3 Comparative and Superlative Forms of Adjectives and Adverbs

	Comparative		Superlative	
ONE-SYLLABLE ADJECTIVES	old wise	older wiser	the oldest the wisest	For most one-syllable adjectives, **-er** and **-est** are added.
TWO-SYLLABLE ADJECTIVES	famous pleasant	more famous more pleasant	the most famous the most pleasant	For most two-syllable adjectives, **more** and **most** are used.
	clever gentle friendly	cleverer more clever gentler more gentle friendlier more friendly	the cleverest the most clever the gentlest the most gentle the friendliest the most friendly	Some two-syllable adjectives use either **-er/-est** or **more/most**: able, angry, clever, common, cruel, friendly, gentle, handsome, narrow, pleasant, polite, quiet, simple, sour.
	busy pretty	busier prettier	the busiest the prettiest	**-Er** and **-est** are used with two-syllable adjectives that end in **-y**. The **-y** is changed to **-i**.
ADJECTIVES WITH THREE OR MORE SYLLABLES	important fascinating	more important more fascinating	the most important the most fascinating	**More** and **most** are used with long adjectives.
IRREGULAR ADJECTIVES	good bad	better worse	the best the worst	**Good** and **bad** have irregular comparative and superlative forms.
-LY ADVERBS	carefully slowly	more carefully more slowly	the most carefully the most slowly	**More** and **most** are used with adverbs that end in **-ly**.*
ONE-SYLLABLE ADVERBS	fast hard	faster harder	the fastest the hardest	The **-er** and **-est** forms are used with one-syllable adverbs.
IRREGULAR ADVERBS	well badly far	better worse farther/further	the best the worst the farthest/furthest	Both **farther** and **further** are used to compare physical distances: *I walked farther than my friend did.* OR *I walked further than my friend did.* **Further** also means "additional": *I need further information.* NOTE: **Farther** cannot be used when the meaning is "additional."

*Exception: **early** is both an adjective and an adverb. Forms: *earlier, earliest.*

❑ **Exercise 10. Looking at grammar.** (Charts 9-2 and 9-3)
Write the comparative and superlative forms of the following adjectives and adverbs.

1. high   _higher, the highest_   8. dangerous _____

2. good   _____   9. slowly   _____

3. lazy   _____   10. common   _____

4. hot★   _____   11. friendly   _____

5. neat★   _____   12. careful   _____

6. late★   _____   13. bad   _____

7. happy   _____   14. far   _____

❑ **Exercise 11. Looking at grammar.** (Charts 9-2 and 9-3)
Complete the sentences with the correct comparative form (**more/-er**) of the adjectives in the list.

clean	dangerous	funny	✓sweet
confusing	dark	pretty	wet

1. Oranges are ___sweeter___ than lemons.

2. I heard some polite laughter when I told my jokes, but everyone laughed loudly when Janet told hers. Her jokes are always much _____ than mine.

3. Many more people die in car accidents than in plane accidents. Statistics show that driving your own car is _____ than flying in an airplane.

4. Professor Sato speaks clearly, but I have trouble understanding Professor Larson's lectures. Her lectures are much _____ than Professor Sato's.

5. Is there a storm coming? The sky looks _____ than it did an hour ago.

6. That tablecloth has some stains on it. Take this one. It's _____.

7. We're having another beautiful sunrise. It looks like an orange fireball. The sky is even _____ than yesterday.

8. If a cat and a duck are out in the rain, the cat will get much _____ than the duck. The water will just roll off the duck's feathers, but it will soak into the cat's hair.

★Spelling notes:
• When a one-syllable adjective ends in *one vowel + a consonant*, double the consonant and add **-er/-est**: *sad, sadder, saddest.*
• When an adjective ends in two *vowels + a consonant*, do NOT double the consonant: **cool, cooler, coolest.**
• When an adjective ends in **-e**, do NOT double the consonant: **wide, wider, widest.**

Exercise 12. Listening. (Chart 9-3)

Listen to the sentences and choose the words that you hear.

Example: You will hear: I am the shortest person in our family.

You will choose: short   shorter   ⟨shortest⟩

My family

1. young	younger	youngest
2. tall	taller	tallest
3. happy	happier	happiest
4. happy	happier	happiest
5. old	older	oldest
6. funny	funnier	funniest
7. hard	harder	hardest
8. hard	harder	hardest

❏ **Exercise 13. Looking at grammar.** (Chart 9-3)

Choose the correct completion(s) for each sentence.

1. Ron and his friend went jogging. Ron ran two miles, but his friend got tired after one
   mile. Ron ran _____ than his friend did.
   ⟨a.⟩ farther   ⟨b.⟩ further

2. If you have any _____ questions, don't hesitate to ask.
   a. farther   b. further

3. I gave my old computer to my younger sister because I had no _____ use for it.
   a. farther   b. further

4. Paris is _____ north than Tokyo.
   a. farther   b. further

5. I like my new apartment, but it is _____ away from school than my old apartment was.
   a. farther   b. further

6. Thank you for your help, but I'll be fine now. I don't want to cause you any _____ trouble.
   a. farther   b. further

7. Which is _____ from here: the subway or the train station?
   a. farther   b. further

❑ **Exercise 14. Let's talk: pairwork.** (Charts 9-2 and 9-3)

Work with a partner. Make comparison sentences with *more/-er* and adjectives in the list. Share some of your answers with the class.

beautiful	enjoyable	light	soft
cheap	expensive	relaxing	stressful
deep	fast	shallow	thick
easy	heavy	short	thin

1. traveling by air \ traveling by train
   → *Traveling by air is faster than traveling by train.*
   → *Traveling by air is more stressful than traveling by train.*
      Etc.
2. a pool \ a lake
3. an elephant's neck \ a giraffe's neck
4. taking a trip \ staying home
5. iron \ wood
6. going to the doctor \ going to the dentist
7. gold \ silver
8. rubber \ wood
9. an emerald \ a diamond
10. a feather \ a blade of grass

❑ **Exercise 15. Listening.** (Charts 9-1 → 9-3)

Listen to each sentence and choose the statement (a. or b.) that has a similar meaning.

Example: You will hear: I need help! Please come as soon as possible.
          You will choose: (a.) Please come quickly.
                            b. Please come when you have time.

1. a. Business is better this year.
   b. Business is worse this year.

2. a. Steven is a very friendly person.
   b. Steven is an unfriendly person.

3. a. The test was difficult for Sam.
   b. The test wasn't so difficult for Sam.

4. a. We can go farther.
   b. We can't go farther.

5. a. Jon made a very good decision.
   b. Jon made a very bad decision.

6. a. I'm going to drive faster.
   b. I'm not going to drive faster.

7. a. Your work was careful.
   b. Your work was not careful.

8. a. I am full.
   b. I would like more to eat.

9. a. My drive and my flight take
      the same amount of time.
   b. My drive takes more time.

Exercise 16. Warm-up. (Chart 9-4)
Complete the sentences with the names of people you know. Make true statements.

1. I'm older than _____ is.

2. I live nearer to/farther from school than _____ does.

3. I got to class earlier/later than _____ did.

4. _____'s hair is longer/shorter than mine.

9-4 Completing a Comparative

(a) I'm older *than **my brother*** (*is*). (b) I'm older *than **he** is.* (c) I'm older *than **him***. (*informal*)	In formal English, a subject pronoun (e.g., *he*) follows ***than***, as in (b). In everyday, informal spoken English, an object pronoun (e.g., *him*) often follows ***than***, as in (c).
(d) He works harder *than I **do**.* (e) I arrived earlier *than they **did**.*	Frequently an auxiliary verb follows the subject after ***than***. In (d): *than I do = than I work*
(f) *Ann's* hair is longer *than **Kate's**.* (g) *Jack's* apartment is smaller *than **mine***.	A possessive noun (e.g., *Kate's*) or pronoun (e.g., *mine*) may follow ***than***.

□ **Exercise 17. Looking at grammar.** (Chart 9-4)
Complete the sentences. Use pronouns in the completions.

1. My sister is only six. She's much younger than ___*I am* OR (informally) *me*___.

2. Peggy is thirteen, and she feels sad. She thinks most of the other girls in school are far more popular than _____.

3. The kids can't lift that heavy box, but Mr. El-Sayid can. He's stronger than

   _____.

4. Jared isn't a very good speller. I can spell much better than _____.

5. I was on time. Carlo was late. I got there earlier than _____.

6. Mariko is out of shape. I can run a lot faster and farther than _____.

7. Isabel's classes are difficult, but my classes are easy. Isabel's classes are more difficult than _____. My classes are easier than _____.

8. Our neighbor's house is very large. Our house is much smaller than

   _____. Their house is larger than _____.

Exercise 18. Warm-up. (Chart 9-5)
Do you agree or disagree with these statements? Circle *yes* or *no*.

1. I enjoy very cold weather.   yes   no
2. It's cooler today than yesterday.   yes   no
3. It's much warmer today than yesterday.   yes   no
4. It's a little hotter today than yesterday.   yes   no

9-5 Modifying Comparatives

(a) Tom is *very old*. (b) Ann drives *very carefully*.	*Very* often modifies adjectives, as in (a), and adverbs, as in (b).
(c) INCORRECT: *Tom is very older than I am.* 　　 INCORRECT: *Ann drives very more carefully* 　　　　　　　　　*than she used to.*	*Very* is NOT used to modify comparative adjectives and adverbs.
(d) Tom is *much / a lot / far older* than I am. (e) Ann drives *much / a lot / far more carefully* than she used to.	Instead, *much*, *a lot*, or *far* are used to modify comparative adjectives and adverbs, as in (d) and (e).
(f) Ben is *a little (bit) older* than I am OR (*informally*) me.	Another common modifier is *a little/a little bit*, as in (f).

❑ **Exercise 19. Looking at grammar.** (Chart 9-5)
Add *very*, *much*, *a lot*, or *far* to the sentences.

1. It's hot today. → It's **very** *hot today*.
2. It's hotter today than yesterday. → It's **much/a lot/far** *hotter today than yesterday*.
3. An airplane is fast.
4. Taking an airplane is faster than driving.
5. Learning a second language is difficult for many people.
6. Learning a second language is more difficult than learning chemistry formulas.
7. You can live more inexpensively in student housing than in a rented apartment.
8. You can live inexpensively in student housing.

❑ **Exercise 20. Warm-up.** (Chart 9-6)
Complete the sentences with your own words.

1. Compare the cost of two cars:

   (*A/An*) _____ is more expensive than (*a/an*) _____ .

2. Compare the cost of two kinds of fruit:

   _____ are less expensive than _____ .

3. Compare the cost of two kinds of shoes (boots, sandals, tennis shoes, flip-flops, etc.):

   _____ are not as expensive as _____ .

4. Compare the cost of two kinds of heat: (gas, electric, solar, wood, coal, etc.):

_____ heat is not as cheap as _____ heat.

9-6 Comparisons with *Less ... Than* and *Not As ... As*

MORE THAN ONE SYLLABLE: (a) A pen is *less expensive than* a book. (b) A pen is *not as expensive as* a book.	The opposite of *-er/more* is expressed by *less* or *not as ... as.* Examples (a) and (b) have the same meaning.
	Less and *not as ... as* are used with adjectives and adverbs of **more than one syllable**.
ONE SYLLABLE: (c) A pen is *not as large as* a book. *INCORRECT:* A pen is less large than a book.	Only *not as ... as* (NOT *less*) is used with **one-syllable adjectives or adverbs**, as in (c).

☐ **Exercise 21. Looking at grammar.** (Chart 9-6)
Circle the correct completion(s) for each sentence.

1. My nephew is _____ old _____ my niece.
    a. less ... than   b. not as ... as

2. My nephew is _____ hard-working _____ my niece.
    a. less ... than   b. not as ... as

3. A bee is _____ big _____ a bird.
    a. less ... than   b. not as ... as

4. My brother is _____ interested in computers _____ I am.
    a. less ... than   b. not as ... as

5. Some students are _____ serious about their schoolwork _____ others.
    a. less ... than   b. not as ... as

6. I am _____ good at repairing things _____ Diane is.
    a. less ... than   b. not as ... as

☐ **Exercise 22. Game.** (Charts 9-1 → 9-6)
Work in teams. Compare the given words using (*not*) *as ... as, less,* and *more/-er.* How many comparison sentences can you think of? The team with the most correct sentences wins.

Example: trees and flowers (*big, colorful, useful, etc.*)
    → *Trees are bigger than flowers.*
    → *Flowers are usually more colorful than trees.*
    → *Flowers are less useful than trees.*
    → *Flowers aren't as tall as trees.*

1. the sun and the moon
2. teenagers and adults
3. two restaurants in this area
4. two famous people in the world

❏ **Exercise 23. Listening.** (Charts 9-1 → 9-6)

Listen to each sentence and the statements that follow it. Choose "T" for true or "F" for false.

Example: France \ Brazil

You will hear: a. France isn't as large as Brazil.

You will choose: Ⓣ   F

You will hear: b. France is bigger than Brazil.

You will choose: T   Ⓕ

1. a sidewalk \ a road
   a. T   F
   b. T   F

2. a hill \ a mountain
   a. T   F
   b. T   F

3. a mountain path \ a mountain peak
   a. T   F
   b. T   F

4. toes \ fingers
   a. T   F
   b. T   F
   c. T   F

5. basic math \ algebra
   a. T   F
   b. T   F
   c. T   F
   d. T   F

❏ **Exercise 24. Warm-up: trivia.** (Chart 9-7)

Compare Manila, Seattle, and Singapore. Which two cities have more rain in December?*

_____ and _____ have more rain

than _____ in December.

9-7 Using *More* with Nouns	
(a) Would you like some *more coffee?* (b) Not everyone is here. I expect *more people* to come later.	In (a): ***Coffee*** is a noun. When ***more*** is used with nouns, it often has the meaning of "additional." It is not necessary to use ***than***.
(c) There are *more people* in China *than* there are in the United States.	***More*** is also used with nouns to make complete comparisons by adding ***than***.
(d) Do you have enough coffee, or would you like some *more?*	When the meaning is clear, the noun may be omitted and ***more*** can be used by itself.

*See *Trivia Answers,* p. 411.

❑ **Exercise 25. Game: trivia.** (Chart 9-7)
Work in teams. Write true sentences using the given information. The team with the most correct sentences wins.*

1. more kinds of mammals: South Africa \ Kenya
   → *Kenya has more kinds of mammals than South Africa.*
2. more volcanoes: Indonesia \ Japan
3. more moons: Saturn \ Venus
4. more people: Saõ Paulo, Brazil \ New York City
5. more islands: Greece \ Finland
6. more mountains: Switzerland \ Nepal
7. more sugar (per 100 grams): an apple \ a banana
8. more fat (per 100 grams): the dark meat of a chicken \ the white meat of a chicken

❑ **Exercise 26. Looking at grammar.** (Charts 9-2, 9-3, and 9-7)
First, underline the words in the list that are nouns. Second, use *-er/more* and the words in the list to complete the sentences.

doctors	information	responsible
happily	mistakes	responsibly
happiness	responsibilities	✓traffic
happy		

1. A city has ___more traffic___ than a small town.

2. There is _____ available on the Internet today than there was one year ago.

3. I used to be sad, but now I'm a lot _____ about my life than I used to be.

4. Unhappy roommates can live together _____ if they learn to respect each other's differences.

5. Maggie's had a miserable year. I hope she finds _____ in the future.

6. I made _____ on the last test than I did on the first one, so I got a worse grade.

7. My daughter Layla is trustworthy and mature. She behaves much _____ than my nephew Jakob.

8. A twelve-year-old has _____ at home and in school than an eight-year-old.

9. My son is _____ about doing his homework than his older sister is.

10. Health care in rural areas is poor. We need _____ to treat people in rural areas.

---

*See *Trivia Answers*, p. 421.

Exercise 27. Warm-up. (Chart 9-8)

Do you agree or disagree with these statements? Circle *yes* or *no*.

1. The grammar in this book is getting harder and harder.	yes	no
2. The assignments in this class are getting longer and longer.	yes	no
3. My English is getting better and better.	yes	no

9-8 Repeating a Comparative

(a) Because he was afraid, he walked *faster and faster*.	Repeating a comparative gives the idea that something becomes progressively greater, i.e., it increases in intensity, quality, or quantity.
(b) Life in the modern world is getting *more and more complicated*.	

❑ **Exercise 28. Looking at grammar.** (Chart 9-8)

Complete the sentences by repeating a comparative. Use the words in the list.

big	✓fast	hard	loud	warm
discouraged	good	long	tired	wet

1. When I get excited, my heart beats ___*faster and faster*___ .

2. When you blow up a balloon, it gets _____ .

3. Brian's health is improving. It's getting _____ every day.

4. As the ambulance came closer to us, the siren became _____ .

5. The line of people waiting to get into the theater got _____ _____ until it went around the building.

6. Thank goodness winter is over. The weather is getting _____ _____ with each passing day.

7. I've been looking for a job for a month and still haven't been able to find one. I'm getting _____ .

8. The rain started as soon as I left my office. As I walked to the bus stop, it rained _____ , and I got _____ .

9. I started to row the boat across the lake, but my arms got _____ _____ , so I turned back.

❑ **Exercise 29. Warm-up.** (Chart 9-9)
Do you agree or disagree with the following idea? Why?

> If you pay more money for something, you will get better quality. In other words, the more expensive something is, the better the quality will be.

9-9 Using Double Comparatives

(a) *The harder* you study, *the more* you will learn. (b) *The more* she studied, *the more* she learned. (c) *The warmer* the weather (is), *the better* I like it.	A double comparative has two parts; both parts begin with *the*, as in the examples. The second part of the comparison is the **result** of the first part. In (a): If you study harder, the result will be that you will learn more.
(d) — Should we ask Jenny and Jim to the party too? — Why not? *The more, the merrier.* (e) — When should we leave? — *The sooner, the better.*	*The more, the merrier* and *the sooner, the better* are two common expressions. In (d): It is good to have more people at the party. In (e): It is good if we leave as soon as we can.

❑ **Exercise 30. Looking at grammar.** (Chart 9-9)
Part I. Complete the sentences with double comparatives (*the more/-er ... the more/-er*) and the words in *italics*.

1. If the fruit is *fresh,* it tastes *good.*

   __The fresher__ the fruit (is), __the better__ it tastes.

2. We got *close* to the fire. We felt *warm.*

   _____ we got to the fire, _____ we felt.

3. If a knife is *sharp,* it is *easy* to cut something with.

   _____ a knife (is), _____ it is to cut something.

4. The party got *noisy* next door. I got *angry.*

   _____ it got, _____ I got.

5. If a flamingo eats a lot of *shrimp,* it becomes very *pink.*

   The _____ a flamingo eats,

   the _____ it gets.

SHRIMP,
ALL YOU
CAN EAT

Part II. Combine each pair of sentences. Use double comparatives (*the more/-er . . . the more/-er*) and the words in *italics*.

6. She drove *fast*. \ I became *nervous*.

    Rosa offered to take me to the airport, and I was grateful. But we got a late start, so she began to drive faster. → *The* faster she drove, *the* more nervous I became.

7. He *thought* about his family. \ He became *homesick*.

    Pierre tried to concentrate on his studies, but he kept thinking about his family and home. →

8. The sky grew *dark*. \ We ran *fast* to reach the house.

    A storm was threatening. →

❑ **Exercise 31. Warm-up.** (Chart 9-10)
Complete the sentences with your own ideas.

1. _____ is the most expensive city I have ever visited.

2. _____ is one of the most expensive cities in the world.

3. _____ is one of the least expensive cities in the world.

9-10 Using Superlatives

(a) Tokyo is one of *the largest cities in the world.* (b) David is *the most generous person I have ever known.* (c) I have three books. These two are quite good, but this one is the *best* (book) *of all.*	Typical completions when a superlative is used: In (a): *superlative* + *in* a place (*the world, this class, my family, the corporation, etc.*) In (b): *superlative* + *adjective clause** In (c): *superlative* + *of all*
(d) I took four final exams. The final in accounting was *the least difficult* of all.	*The least* has the opposite meaning of *the most.*
(e) Ali is *one of* the best *students* in this class. (f) *One of* the best *students* in this class *is* Ali.	Notice the pattern with *one of:* *one of* + *plural noun* (+ *singular verb*)
(g) I've *never* taken a *harder* test. (h) I've *never* taken a *hard* test.	*Never* + comparative = superlative Example (g) means "It was the hardest test I've ever taken." Compare (g) and (h).

*See Chapter 12 for more information about adjective clauses.

❑ **Exercise 32. Looking at grammar.** (Chart 9-10)
Complete the sentences with superlatives of the words in *italics* and the appropriate preposition, *in* or *of*.

1. Kyle is *lazy*. He is ___the laziest___ student ___in___ the class.

2. Mike and Julie were *nervous*, but Amanda was ___the most nervous of___ all.

3. Costa Rica is *beautiful*. It is one of _____
   countries _____ the world.

4. Scott got a *bad* score on the test. It was one of _____ scores
   _____ the class.

5. Neptune is *far* from the sun. Is it _____ planet from the
   sun _____ our solar system?

6. There are a lot of *good* cooks in my family, but my mom is _____ cook
   _____ all.

7. My grandfather is very *old*. He is _____ person _____ the town
   where he lives.

8. That chair in the corner is *comfortable*. It is _____
   chair _____ the room.

9. Everyone who ran in the race was *exhausted*, but I was _____ all.

❑ **Exercise 33. Looking at grammar.** (Chart 9-10)
Complete the sentences with the superlative form of the given phrases.

big bird	long river in South America
two great natural dangers	popular forms of entertainment
✓deep ocean	three common street names
high mountains on earth	

1. The Pacific is ___the deepest ocean___ in the world.

2. _____ are in the Himalayan Range
   in Asia.

3. Most birds are small, but not the flightless North African ostrich. It is
   _____ in the world.

4. _____ to ships are fog and icebergs.

5. One of _____ throughout the world
   is movies.

6. _____ in the United States are Park,
   Washington, and Maple.

7. _____ is the Amazon.

❑ **Exercise 34. Looking at grammar.** (Chart 9-10)
Complete the sentences with the superlative form of the words in *italics*.

1. I have had many *good experiences*. Of those, my vacation to Honduras was one of
_____ I have ever had.

2. Ayako has had many *nice times,* but her birthday party was one of _____
_____ she has ever had.

3. I've taken many *difficult courses,* but statistics is one of _____
_____ I've ever taken.

4. I've made some *bad mistakes* in my life, but lending money to my cousin was one of
_____ I've ever made.

5. We've seen many *beautiful buildings* in the world, but the Taj Mahal is one of _____
_____ I've ever seen.

6. The *final exam* I took was pretty *easy*. In fact, it was one of _____
_____ I've ever taken.

❑ **Exercise 35. Let's talk: pairwork.** (Chart 9-10)
Work with a partner. Take turns asking and answering questions. Use superlatives in your
answers. Pay special attention to the use of plural nouns after **one of**.

Example:
SPEAKER A: You have known many interesting people. Who is one of them?
SPEAKER B: **One of the most interesting people** I've ever known **is** (_____). OR
(_____) **is one of the most interesting people** I've ever known.

1. There are many beautiful countries in the world. What is one of them?
2. There are many famous people in the world. Who is one of them?
3. You've probably seen many good movies. What is one of them?
4. You've probably done many interesting things in your life. What is one of them?
5. Think of some happy days in your life. What was one of them?
6. There are a lot of interesting animals in the world. What is one of them?
7. You have probably had many good experiences. What is one of them?
8. You probably know several funny people. Who is one of them?

❑ **Exercise 36. Grammar and listening.** (Chart 9-10)
Part I. Circle the sentence (a. or b.) that is closest in meaning to the given sentence.

1. I've never been on a bumpier plane ride.
   a. The flight was bumpy.   b. The flight wasn't bumpy.

2. I've never tasted hot chili peppers.
   a. The peppers are hot.   b. I haven't eaten hot chili peppers.

3. The house has never looked cleaner.
   - a. The house looks clean.
   - b. The house doesn't look clean.

4. We've never visited a more beautiful city.
   - a. The city was beautiful.
   - b. The city wasn't beautiful.

Part II. Listen to the sentences. Circle the sentence (a. or b.) that is closest in meaning to the one you hear.

5. a. His jokes are funny.   b. His jokes aren't funny.

6. a. It tastes great.   b. It doesn't taste very good.

7. a. The mattress is hard.   b. I haven't slept on hard mattresses.

8. a. The movie was scary.   b. I haven't watched scary movies.

❑ **Exercise 37. Let's talk: interview.** (Chart 9-10)
Make questions with the given words and the superlative form, and then interview your classmates. Share some of their answers with the class.

1. what \ bad movie \ you have ever seen
   → *What is the worst movie you have ever seen?*
2. what \ interesting sport to watch \ on TV
3. what \ crowded city \ you have ever visited
4. where \ good restaurant to eat \ around here
5. what \ fun place to visit \ in this area
6. who \ kind person \ you know
7. what \ important thing \ in life
8. what \ serious problem \ in the world
9. who \ most interesting person \ in the news right now

❑ **Exercise 38. Game.** (Charts 9-1 → 9-10)
Work in teams. Compare each list of items using the words in *italics*. Write sentences using *as . . . as*, the comparative (*-er/more*), and the superlative (*-est/most*). The group with the most correct sentences wins.

Example: streets in this city: *wide / narrow / busy / dangerous*
   → *First Avenue is **wider** than Market Street.*
   → *Second Avenue is **nearly as wide as** First Avenue.*
   → *First Avenue is **narrower** than Interstate Highway 70.*
   → ***The busiest** street is Main Street.*
   → *Main Street is **busier** than Market Street.*
   → ***The most dangerous street** in the city is Olive Boulevard.*

1. a lemon, a grapefruit, and an orange: *sweet / sour / large / small*
2. a kitten, a cheetah, and a lion: *weak / powerful / wild / gentle / fast*
3. boxing, soccer, and golf: *dangerous / safe / exciting / boring*
4. the food at (*three places in this city where you have eaten*): *delicious / appetizing / inexpensive / good / bad*

❑ **Exercise 39. Looking at grammar.** (Charts 9-1 → 9-10)
Complete the sentences with any appropriate form of the words in parentheses. Add any other necessary words. In some cases, more than one completion may be possible.

1. Lead is a very heavy metal. It is (*heavy*) __heavier than__ gold or silver. It is one of (*heavy*) __the heaviest__ metals __of__ all.

2. Mrs. Cook didn't ask the children to clean up the kitchen. It was (*easy*) _____ for her to do it herself _____ to nag them to do it.

3. A car has two (*wheels*) _____ a bicycle.

4. Crocodiles and alligators are different. The snout of a crocodile is (*long*) _____ and (*narrow*) _____ than an alligator's snout. An alligator has a (*wide*) _____ upper jaw than a crocodile.

5. Although both jobs are important, being a teacher requires (*education*) _____ _____ being a bus driver.

6. The Great Wall of China is (*long*) _____ structure that has ever been built.

7. Hannah Anderson is one of (*friendly*) _____ and (*delightful*) _____ people I've ever met.

8. One of (*famous*) _____ volcanoes _____ the world is Mount Etna in Sicily.

9. It's possible that the volcanic explosion of Krakatoa near Java in 1883 was (*loud*) _____ noise _____ recorded history. People heard it 2,760 miles/4,441 kilometers away.

10. (*hard*) _____ I tried, (*impossible*) _____ the math problem seemed.

11. World Cup Soccer is (*big*) _____ sporting event _____ the world. It is viewed on TV by (*people*) _____ any other event in sports.

12. When the temperature stays below freezing for a long period of time, the Eiffel Tower becomes six inches or fifteen centimeters (*short*) _____ .

13. Young people have (*high*) _____ rate of automobile accidents _____ all drivers.

14. You'd better buy the tickets for the show soon. (*long*) _____ you wait, (*difficult*) _____ it will be for you to get good seats.

15. No animals can travel (*fast*) _____ birds. Birds are (*fast*) _____ animals of all.

16. (*great*) _____ variety of birds _____ a single area can be found in the rainforests of Southeast Asia and India.

❑ **Exercise 40. Warm-up.** (Chart 9-11)
Solve the math problems* and then complete the sentences.

Problem A: $2 + 2 =$
Problem B: $\sqrt{900} + 20 =$
Problem C: $3 \times 127 =$
Problem D: $2 + 3 =$
Problem E: $127 \times 3 =$

1. Problem ____ and Problem ____ have the same answers.

2. Problem ____ and Problem ____ have similar answers

3. Problem ____ and Problem ____ have different answers.

4. The answer to Problem ____ is the same as the answer to Problem ____ .

5. The answers to Problem ____ and Problem ____ are similar.

6. The answers to Problem ____ Problem ____ are different.

7. Problem ____ has the same answer as Problem ____ .

8. Problem ____ is like Problem ____ .

9. Problem ____ and Problem ____ are alike.

*See *Trivia Answers*, p. 421, for answers to the math problems.

9-11 Using *The Same, Similar, Different, Like, Alike*

(a) John and Mary have *the same books*. (b) John and Mary have *similar books*. (c) John and Mary have *different books*. (d) Their books are *the same*. (e) Their books are *similar*. (f) Their books are *different*.	*The same*, *similar*, and *different* are used as adjectives. Notice: *the* always precedes *same*.
(g) This book is *the same as* that one. (h) This book is *similar to* that one. (i) This book is *different from* that one.	Notice: *the same* is followed by *as*; *similar* is followed by *to*; *different* is followed by *from*.*
(j) She is *the same age as* my mother. My shoes are *the same size as* yours.	A noun may come between *the same* and *as*, as in (j).
(k) My pen *is like* your pen. (l) My pen *and* your pen *are alike*.	Notice in (k) and (l): *noun* + *be like* + *noun* *noun* **and** *noun* + *be alike*
(m) She *looks like* her sister. It *looks like* rain. It *sounds like* thunder. This material *feels like* silk. That *smells like* gas. This chemical *tastes like* salt. Stop *acting like* a fool. He *seems like* a nice guy.	In addition to following *be*, *like* also follows certain verbs, primarily those dealing with the senses. Notice the examples in (m).
(n) The twins *look alike*. We *think alike*. Most four-year-olds *act alike*. My sister and I *talk alike*. The little boys are *dressed alike*.	*Alike* may follow a few verbs other than *be*. Notice the examples in (n).

*In informal speech, native speakers might use *than* instead of *from* after *different*. *From* is considered correct in formal English, unless the comparison is completed by a clause: *I have a different attitude now than I used to have.*

❑ **Exercise 41. Looking at grammar.** (Chart 9-11)
Complete the sentences with *as, to, from,* or *Ø*.

1. Geese are similar __to__ ducks. They are both large water birds.

2. But geese are not the same _____ ducks. Geese are usually larger and have longer necks.

3. Geese are different _____ ducks.

4. Geese are like _____ ducks in some ways, but geese and ducks are not exactly alike _____.

5. An orange is similar _____ a peach. They are both round, sweet, and juicy.

6. However, an orange is not the same _____ a peach.

7. An orange is different _____ a peach.

8. An orange is like _____ a peach in some ways, but they are not exactly alike _____ .

❑ **Exercise 42. Listening.** (Charts 9-3 and 9-11)
Listen to each passage. Complete the sentences with the words you hear.

Gold vs. Silver

Gold is similar _____ silver. They are both valuable metals that people use for

₁

jewelry, but they aren't _____ same. Gold is not _____ same color

₂
₃

_____ silver. Gold is also different _____ silver in cost: gold is

₄
₅

_____ expensive _____ silver.

₆
₇

Two Zebras

Look at the two zebras in the picture. Their names are Zee and Bee. Zee looks

_____ Bee. Is Zee exactly _____ same _____ Bee? The pattern of

₈
₉
₁₀

the stripes on each zebra in the world is unique. No two zebras are exactly _____ .

₁₁

Even though Zee and Bee are similar _____ each other, they are different

₁₂

_____ each other in the exact pattern of their stripes.

₁₃

❑ **Exercise 43. Looking at grammar.** (Chart 9-11)
Compare the figures. Complete the sentences with *the same* (*as*), *similar* (*to*), *different* (*from*), *like,* or *alike.*

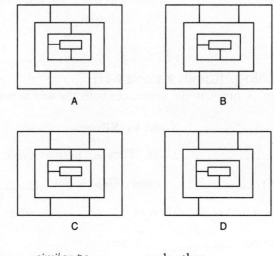

1. All of the figures are __similar to__ each other.

2. Figure A is _____ Figure B.

3. Figure A and Figure B are _____.

4. A and C are _____.

5. A and C are _____ D.

6. C is _____ A.

7. B isn't _____ D.

❑ **Exercise 44. Looking at grammar.** (Chart 9-11)
Complete the sentences with *the same* (*as*), *similar* (*to*), *different* (*from*), *like,* or *alike.* In some cases, more than one completion may be possible.

1. Jennifer and Jack both come from Rapid City. In other words, they come from
   __the same__ town.

2. This city is __the same as / similar to / like__ my hometown. Both are quiet and conservative.

3. You and I don't agree. Your ideas are _____ mine.

4. Sergio never wears _____ clothes two days in a row.

5. A male mosquito is not _____ size _____ a female mosquito. The female is larger.

6. I'm used to stronger coffee. I think the coffee at this cafe tastes _____ dishwater!

7. *Meet* and *meat* are homonyms; in other words, they have _____ pronunciation.

8. *Flower* has _____ pronunciation _____ *flour.*

9. My twin sisters act _____, but they don't look _____.

10. Trying to get through school without studying is _____ trying to go swimming without getting wet.

❑ **Exercise 45. Reading.** (Chapter 9)
Part I. Read the passage and the statements that follow it. NOTE: *He* and *she* are used interchangeably.

Birth Order

In your family, are you the oldest, youngest, middle, or only child? Some psychologists believe your place in the family, or your birth order, has a strong influence on your personality. Let's look at some of the personality characteristics of each child.

The oldest child has all the parents' attention when she is born. As she grows up, she may want to be the center of attention. Because she is around adults, she might act more like an adult around other children and be somewhat controlling. As the oldest, she might have to take care of the younger children, so she may be more responsible. She may want to be the leader when she is in groups.

The middle child (or children) may feel a little lost. Middle children have to share their parents' attention. They may try to be different from the oldest child. If the oldest child is "good," the second child may be "bad." However, since they need to get along with both the older and younger sibling(s), they may be the peacekeepers of the family.

The youngest child is the "baby" of the family. Other family members may see him as weaker, smaller, or more helpless. If the parents know this is their last child, they may not want the child to grow up as quickly as the other children. As a way to get attention, the youngest child may be the funniest child in the family. He may also have more freedom and turn out to be more artistic and creative.

An only child (no brothers or sisters) often grows up in an adult world. Such children may use adult language and prefer adult company. Only children may be more intelligent and serious than other children their age. They might also be more self-centered because of all the attention they get, and they might have trouble sharing with others.

Of course, these are general statements. A lot depends on how the parents raise the child, how many years are between each child, and the culture the child grows up in. How about you? Do you see any similarities to your family?

Part II. Read the statements. Circle "T" for true and "F" for false according to the information in the passage.

1. The two most similar children are the oldest and only child.   T   F

2. The middle child often wants to be like the oldest child.   T   F

3. The youngest child likes to control others.   T   F

4. Only children may want to spend time with adults.   T   F

5. All cultures share the same birth order characteristics.   T   F

❑ **Exercise 46. Writing.** (Chapter 9)

Part I. The word list contains personality characteristics. Do you know all these words?

artistic	funny	rebellious
competitive	hard-working	relaxed
controlling	immature	secretive
cooperative	loud	sensitive
creative	mature	serious
flexible	outgoing	shy

Part II. Compare yourself to other members of your family. Write sentences using the structures below:

Structures:

1. not as . . . as
2. more . . . than
3. -er . . . than
4. the most . . .

Part III. Write a paragraph comparing your personality to that of another member of your family. Follow these steps:

1. Write an introductory sentence: *I am different from / similar to my . . .*
2. Choose at least four characteristics from the list. For each one, make some type of comparison.
3. Write a few details that explain each comparison.
4. Write one or two concluding sentences.

Sample paragraph:

My Father and I

I am different from my father in several ways. He is more hard-working than I am. He is a construction worker and has to get up at 6:00 A.M. He often doesn't get home until late in the evening. I'm a student, and I don't work as hard. Another difference is that I am funnier than he is. I like to tell jokes and make people laugh. He is serious, but he laughs at my jokes. My father was an athlete when he was my age, and he is very competitive. I don't like playing competitive sports, but we watch them together on TV. My father and I are different, but we like to spend time with each other. Our differences make our time together interesting.

Exercise 47. Check your knowledge. (Chapter 9)
Edit the sentences. Correct the errors in comparison structures

1. Did you notice? My shoes and your shoes are ∅ *the* same.

2. Alaska is largest state in the United States.

3. A pillow is soft, more than a rock.

4. Who is most generous person in your family?

5. The harder you work, you will be more successful.

6. One of a biggest disappointment in my life was when my soccer team lost the championship.

7. My sister is very taller than me.

8. A firm mattress is so comfortable for many people than a soft mattress.

9. One of the most talkative student in the class is Frederick.

10. Professor Bennett's lectures were the confusing I have ever heard.

Chapter 10

The Passive

☐ **Exercise 1. Warm-up.** (Charts 10-1 and 10-2)

Choose the sentence in each item that describes the picture above it. More than one answer may be correct.

1. a. The worm is watching the bird.
   b. The bird is watching the worm.

2. a. The bird caught the worm.
   b. The worm was caught by the bird.

3. a. The bird ate the worm.
   b. The worm was eaten.

10-1 Active Sentences and Passive Sentences

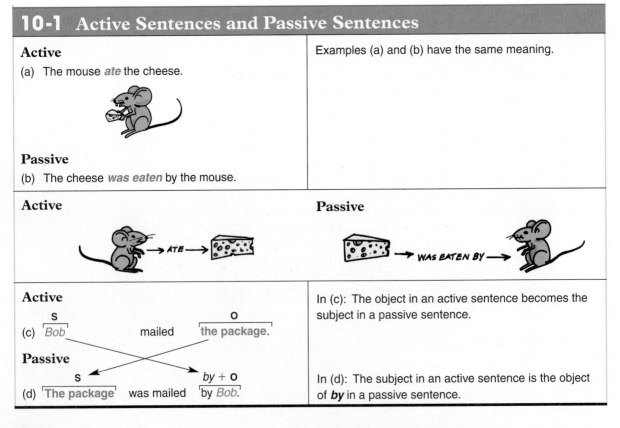

Active	Examples (a) and (b) have the same meaning.
(a) The mouse *ate* the cheese.	
Passive	
(b) The cheese *was eaten* by the mouse.	

Active	Passive

Active	In (c): The object in an active sentence becomes the subject in a passive sentence.
(c) *Bob* mailed the package.	
Passive	In (d): The subject in an active sentence is the object of *by* in a passive sentence.
(d) *The package* was mailed *by Bob.*	

10-2 Form of the Passive

	be +	**past participle**		Form of all passive verbs:
(a) Corn	*is*	*grown*	by farmers.	**be** + *past participle*
(b) Sara	*was*	*surprised*	by the news.	**Be** can be in any of its forms: *am, is, are, was, were,*
(c) The report	*will be*	*written*	by Mary.	*has been, have been, will be, etc.*

	Active	**Passive**
SIMPLE PRESENT	Farmers *grow* corn. ⟶	Corn *is grown* by farmers.
SIMPLE PAST	The news *surprised* Sara. ⟶	Sara *was surprised* by the news.
PRESENT PROGRESSIVE	Diana *is copying* the letters. ⟶	The letters *are being copied* by Diana.
PAST PROGRESSIVE	Diana *was copying* the letters. ⟶	The letters *were being copied* by Diana.
PRESENT PERFECT	Jack *has mailed* the letter. ⟶	The letter *has been mailed* by Jack.
FUTURE	Mr. Lee *will plan* the meeting. ⟶ Sue *is going to write* the report. ⟶	The meeting *will be planned* by Mr. Lee. The report *is going to be written* by Sue.

☐ **Exercise 2. Looking at grammar.** (Charts 10-1 and 10-2)
Change the active verbs to passive by adding the correct form of **be**. Include the subject of the passive sentence.

1. SIMPLE PRESENT

   a. The teacher *helps* **me**.   __I__   __am__   **helped** by the teacher.

   b. The teacher *helps* **Eva**.   __Eva__   __is__   **helped** by the teacher.

   c. The teacher *helps* **us**.   _____   _____   **helped** by the teacher.

2. SIMPLE PAST

   a. The teacher *helped* **him**.   _____   _____   **helped** by the teacher.

   b. The teacher *helped* **them**.   _____   _____   **helped** by the teacher.

3. PRESENT PROGRESSIVE

   a. The teacher *is helping* **us**.   _____   _____   **helped** by the teacher.

   b. The teacher *is helping* **her**.   _____   _____   **helped** by the teacher.

4. PAST PROGRESSIVE

   a. The teacher *was helping* **me**.   _____   _____   **helped** by the teacher.

   b. The teacher *was helping* **him**.   _____   _____   **helped** by the teacher.

5. PRESENT PERFECT

   a. The teacher *has helped* **Yoko**.   _____   _____   **helped** by the teacher.

   b. The teacher *has helped* **Joe**.   _____   _____   **helped** by the teacher.

6. FUTURE
   a. The teacher *will help* **me**.   _____ _____ **helped** by the teacher.
   b. The teacher *is going to help* **us**.   _____ _____ **helped** by the teacher.

□ **Exercise 3. Listening.** (Charts 10-1 and 10-2)
Listen to the sentences and write the words and endings you hear. Listen to the sentences again as you check your answers.

An office building at night

1. The janitors *clean* the building at night.

   The building __*is*__ clean _*ed*_ by the janitors at night.

2. Window washers *wash* the windows.

   The windows _____ wash ____ by window washers.

3. A window washer *is washing* a window right now.

   A window _____ wash ____ by a window washer right now.

4. The security guard *has checked* the offices.

   The offices _____ check ____ by the security guard.

5. The security guard *discovered* an open window.

   An open window _____ discover ____ by the security guard.

6. The security guard *found* an unlocked door.

   An unlocked door _____ found by the security guard.

7. The owner *will visit* the building tomorrow.

   The building _____ visit ____ by the owner tomorrow.

8. The owner *is going to announce* new parking fees.

   New parking fees _____ announce ____ by the owner.

□ **Exercise 4. Looking at grammar.** (Charts 10-1 and 10-2)
Check (✓) the sentences that are passive.

At the dentist

1. _____ The dental assistant cleaned your teeth.
2. _____ Your teeth were cleaned by the dental assistant.
3. _____ The dentist is checking your teeth.
4. _____ Your teeth are being checked by the dentist.
5. _____ You have a cavity.
6. _____ You are going to need a filling.
7. _____ The filling will be done by the dentist.
8. _____ You will need to schedule another appointment.

□ **Exercise 5. Looking at grammar.** (Charts 10-1 and 10-2)
Change the verbs from active to passive. Do not change the tenses.

		be	+	**past participle**	

1. Leo *mailed* the package.   The package _<u>was</u>_ _____<u>mailed</u>_____ by Leo.

2. That company *employs* many people.   Many people _____ _____ by that company.

3. That company *has hired* Ellen.   Ellen _____ _____ by that company.

4. The secretary *is going to fax* the letter.   The letters _____ _____ by the secretary.

5. A college student *bought* my old car.   My old car _____ _____ by a college student.

6. Mrs. Adams *will do* the work.   The work _____ _____ by Mrs. Adams.

7. The doctor *was examining* the patient.   The patient _____ _____ by the doctor.

Exercise 6. Looking at grammar. (Charts 10-1 and 10-2)
Change the sentences from active to passive.

Active	**Passive**	
1. a. The news surprised Carlo.	_____ *Carlo was surprised* _____	by the news.
b. Did the news surprise you?	_____ *Were you surprised* _____	by the news?
2. a. The news surprises Erin.	_____	by the news.
b. Does the news surprise you?	_____	by the news?
3. a. The news will shock Greta.	_____	by the news.
b. Will the news shock Pat?	_____	by the news?
4. a. Liz is signing the birthday card.	_____	by Liz.
b. Is Ricardo signing it?	_____	by Ricardo?
5. a. Jill signed the card.	_____	by Jill.
b. Did Ryan sign it?	_____	by Ryan?
6. a. Sami was signing it.	_____	by Sami.
b. Was Vicki signing it?	_____	by Vicki?
7. a. Rob has signed it.	_____	by Rob.
b. Has Kazu signed it yet?	_____	by Kazu yet?
8. a. Luis is going to sign it.	_____	by Luis.
b. Is Carole going to sign it?	_____	by Carole?

Exercise 7. Looking at grammar. (Charts 10-1 and 10-2)
Change these hotel questions from active to passive.

1. Has the maid cleaned our room yet?
   → *Has our room been cleaned by the maid yet?*
2. Does the hotel provide hair dryers?
3. Did housekeeping bring extra towels?
4. Has room service brought our meal?
5. Is the bellhop* bringing our luggage to our room?
6. Is maintenance going to fix the air-conditioning?
7. Will the front desk upgrade** our room?

---

*bellhop = a person who carries luggage for hotel guests

**upgrade = make better; in this case, provide a better room than the original one. *Upgrade* is a regular verb.

Exercise 8. Warm-up. (Chart 10-3)

Check (✓) the sentences that have objects. <u>Underline</u> the objects.

1. _____ The tree fell over.
2. _____ The tree hit the truck.
3. _____ The tree fell on the truck.
4. _____ Fortunately, the driver didn't die.
5. _____ The tree didn't kill the driver.

10-3 Transitive and Intransitive Verbs

Transitive

	S	V	O
(a)	Bob	*mailed*	*the letter.*
(b)	Mr. Lee	*signed*	*the check.*
(c)	A cat	*killed*	*the bird.*

A TRANSITIVE verb is a verb that is followed by an object. An object is a noun or a pronoun.

Intransitive

	S	V	
(d)	Something	*happened.*	
(e)	Kate	*came*	to our house.
(f)	The bird	*died.*	

An INTRANSITIVE verb is a verb that is NOT followed by an object.

Common Intransitive Verbs*

agree	die	happen	rise	stand
appear	exist	laugh	seem	stay
arrive	fall	live	sit	talk
become	flow	occur	sleep	wait
come	go	rain	sneeze	walk

Transitive Verbs

(g) ACTIVE: Bob *mailed* the letter.

(h) PASSIVE: The letter *was mailed* by Bob.

Only transitive verbs can be used in the passive.

Intransitive Verbs

(i) ACTIVE: Something *happened.*

(j) PASSIVE: (*not possible*)

(k) INCORRECT: Something *was happened.*

An intransitive verb is NOT used in the passive.

*To find out if a verb is transitive or intransitive, look in your dictionary. The usual abbreviations are v.t. (transitive) and v.i. (intransitive). Some verbs have both transitive and intransitive uses. For example:

   transitive: *Students study books.*

   intransitive: *Students study.*

□ **Exercise 9. Looking at grammar.** (Chart 10-3)
Underline the verbs and identify them as transitive (v.t.) or intransitive (v.i.). If possible, change the sentences to the passive.

           v.i.
1. Omar <u>walked</u> to school yesterday. (*no change*)

           v.t.
2. Alexa <u>broke</u> the window. → *The window was broken by Alexa.*

3. The leaves fell to the ground.

4. I slept at my friend's house last night.

5. Many people felt an earthquake yesterday.

6. Dinosaurs existed millions of years ago.

7. I usually agree with my sister.

8. Many people die during a war.

9. Scientists will discover a cure for cancer someday.

10. Did the Italians invent spaghetti?

□ **Exercise 10. Game: trivia.** (Charts 10-1 → 10-3)
Work in teams. Make true statements by matching the information in Column A with the information in Column B. Some sentences are active and some are passive. Add **was/were** as necessary. The team with the most answers wins.★ A sentence is correct when both the facts and the grammar are correct.

Example: 1. Alexander Eiffel **designed** the Eiffel Tower.
          2. Anwar Sadat **was shot** in 1981.

Column A	**Column B**
1. Alexander Eiffel _h_	a. killed in a car crash in 1997.
2. Anwar Sadat _c_	b. died in 2009.
3. Princess Diana ____	✓c. shot in 1981.
4. Marie and Pierre Curie ____	d. painted the *Mona Lisa*.
5. Oil ____	e. elected president of the United States in 1960.
6. Mahatma Gandhi and Martin Luther King Jr. ____	f. discovered in Saudi Arabia in 1938.
	g. arrested★★ several times for peaceful protests.
7. Michael Jackson ____	✓h. designed the Eiffel Tower.
8. Leonardo da Vinci ____	i. released from prison in 1990.
9. John F. Kennedy ____	j. discovered radium.
10. Nelson Mandela ____	

★See *Trivia Answers,* p. 421.

★★*arrested* = taken to jail

❑ **Exercise 11. Warm-up.** (Chart 10-4)
Complete the sentences with information from the front of this book.

1. This book, *Fundamentals of English Grammar,* was published by _____.

2. It was written by _____ and _____.

3. The illustrations were drawn by _____ and _____.

10-4 Using the *by*-Phrase

(a) This sweater *was made* **by my aunt.**	The *by*-phrase is used in passive sentences when it is important to know who performs an action. In (a): **by my aunt** is important information.
(b) My sweater *was made* in Korea. (c) Spanish *is spoken* in Colombia. (d) That house *was built* in 1940. (e) Rice *is grown* in many countries.	Usually there is no *by*-phrase in a passive sentence. The passive is used when it is **not known or not important to know exactly who performs an action**. In (b): The exact person (or people) who made the sweater is not known and is not important to know, so there is no *by*-phrase in the passive sentence.
(f) **My aunt** is very skillful. **She** *made* this sweater. (g) A: I like your sweaters. B: Thanks. **This sweater** *was made by* my aunt. **That sweater** *was made by* my mother.	Usually the active is used when the speaker knows who performed the action, as in (f), where the focus of attention is on **my aunt**. In (g): Speaker B uses the passive WITH a *by*-phrase because he wants to focus attention on the subjects of the sentences. The focus of attention is on the two sweaters. The *by*-phrases add important information.

❑ **Exercise 12. Looking at grammar.** (Chart 10-4)
Change the sentences from active to passive. Include the *by*-phrase only as necessary.

1. Bob Smith built that house.
   → *That house was built by Bob Smith.*

2. Someone built this house in 1904.

3. People grow rice in India.

4. Do people speak Spanish in Peru?

5. Alexander Graham Bell invented the telephone.

6. When did someone invent the first computer?

7. People sell hammers at a hardware store.

8. Has anyone ever hypnotized you?

9. Someone published *The Origin of Species* in 1859.

10. Charles Darwin wrote *The Origin of Species*.

□ **Exercise 13. Looking at grammar.** (Chart 10-4)
Underline the passive verbs in each pair of sentences and then answer the questions.

1. a. The mail is usually delivered to Hamid's apartment around ten o'clock.
   b. The mail carrier usually delivers the mail to Hamid's apartment around ten o'clock.

   QUESTIONS: Is it important to know who delivers the mail? → No.
   Which sentence do you think is more common? → Sentence a.

2. a. Construction workers built our school in the 1980s.
   b. Our school was built in the 1980s.

   QUESTIONS: Is it important to know who built the school?
   Which sentence do you think is more common?

3. a. That office building was designed in 1990.
   b. That office building was designed by an architect in 1990.
   c. That office building was designed by my husband in 1990.

   QUESTIONS: What additional information do the *by*-phrases provide?
   Which sentence has important information in the *by*-phrase?

4. a. *Thailand* means "land of the free."
   b. The country of Thailand has never been ruled by a foreign power.

   QUESTION: What happens to the meaning of the second sentence if there is no
   by-phrase?

□ **Exercise 14. Looking at grammar.** (Charts 10-1 → 10-4)
Make sentences with the given words, either orally or in writing. Some sentences are active
and some are passive. Use the past tense. Do not change the order of the words.

A traffic stop

1. The police \ stop \ a speeding car
   → *The police stopped a speeding car.*

2. The driver \ tell \ to get out of the car \ by the police

3. The driver \ take out \ his license

4. The driver \ give \ his license \ to the police officer

5. The license \ check

6. The driver \ give \ a ticket

7. The driver \ tell \ to drive more carefully

❑ **Exercise 15. Listening.** (Charts 10-1 → 10-4)

Complete the sentences with the words you hear. Before you begin, you may want to check your understanding of these words: *treated, bruises, reckless*.

A bike accident

A: Did you hear about the accident outside the dorm entrance?

B: No. What _____?

                         1

A: A guy on a bike _____ by a taxi.

                            2

B: _____ he _____?

        3   4

A: Yeah. Someone _____ an ambulance. He _____ to

                         5   6

City Hospital and _____ in the emergency room for cuts and

                                 7

bruises.

B: What _____ to the taxi driver?

                        8

A: He _____ for reckless driving.

                     9

B: He's lucky that the bicyclist _____.

                             10

❑ **Exercise 16. Looking at grammar.** (Charts 10-1 → 10-4)

Complete the sentences with the correct form (active or passive) of the verb in parentheses.

1. Yesterday our teacher (*arrive*) __*arrived*__ five minutes late.

2. Last night my favorite TV program (*interrupt*) _____
by breaking news.

3. That's not my coat. It (*belong*) _____ to Lara.

4. Our mail (*deliver*) _____ before noon every day.

5. The "b" in *comb* (*pronounce, not*) _____. It is silent.

6. What (*happen*) _____ to John? Where is he?

7. When I (*arrive*) _____ at the airport yesterday, I (*meet*)
_____ by my cousin and a couple of her friends.

8. Yesterday Lee and I (*hear*) _____ about Scott's divorce. I (*surprise, not*)
_____ by the news, but Lee (*shock*)
_____.

9. A new house (*build*) _____ next to ours next year.

10. Roberto (*write*) _____ that composition last week. This one (*write*)
_____ yesterday.

11. At the soccer game yesterday, the winning goal (*kick*) _____ by Luigi. Over 100,000 people (*attend*) _____ the soccer game.

12. A: I think American football is too violent.

    B: I (*agree*) _____ with you. I (*prefer*) _____ baseball.

13. A: When (*your bike, steal*) _____?

    B: Two days ago.

14. A: (*you, pay*) _____ your electric bill yet?

    B: No, I haven't, but I'd better pay it today. If I don't, my electricity (*shut off*)

    _____ by the power company.

❑ **Exercise 17. Listening.** (Charts 10-1 → 10-4)
Listen to the passage with your book closed. Listen again and complete the sentences with the verbs you hear. Before you begin, you may want to check your understanding of these words: *ancient, athlete, designed, wealthy.*

Swimming Pools

Swimming pools __*are*__ very popular nowadays, but can you guess when swimming
              1

pools _____ first _____? _____ it 100 years ago? Five hundred
              2   3   4

years ago? A thousand years ago? Actually, ancient Romans and Greeks _____
                                                                              5

the first swimming pools. Male athletes and soldiers _____ in them for training.
                                                                  6

Believe it or not, as early as 1 B.C., a heated swimming pool _____ for
                                                                        7

a wealthy Roman. But swimming pools _____ popular until the
                                                  8

middle of the 1800s. The city of London _____ six indoor swimming pools.
                                                  9

Soon after, the modern Olympic games _____, and swimming races _____
                                                  10   11

included in the events. After this, swimming pools _____ even more popular,
                                                          12

and now they _____ all over the world.
                        13

Exercise 18. Warm-up. (Chart 10-5)
Read the paragraph and then the statements. Circle "T" for true and "F" for false.

Getting a Passport

Jerry is applying for a passport. He needs to bring proof of citizenship, two photographs, and the application to the passport office. He also needs money for the fee. He will receive his passport in the mail about three weeks after he applies for it.

1.	The application process can be completed by mail.	T	F
2.	Proof of citizenship must be provided.	T	F
3.	A fee has to be paid.	T	F
4.	Photographs should be taken before Jerry goes to the passport office.	T	F
5.	The passport will be sent by mail.	T	F

10-5 Passive Modal Auxiliaries

Active Modal Auxiliaries	Passive Modal Auxiliaries (*modal* + ***be*** + *past participle*)	Modal auxiliaries are often used in the passive.
Bob *will mail* it. Bob *can mail* it. Bob *should mail* it. Bob *ought to mail* it. Bob *must mail* it. Bob *has to mail* it. Bob *may mail* it. Bob *might mail* it. Bob *could mail* it.	It *will be mailed* by Bob. It *can be mailed* by Bob. It *should be mailed* by Bob. It *ought to be mailed* by Bob. It *must be mailed* by Bob. It *has to be mailed* by Bob. It *may be mailed* by Bob. It *might be mailed* by Bob. It *could be mailed* by Bob.	FORM: *modal* + ***be*** + *past participle* (See Chapter 7 for information about the meanings and uses of modal auxiliaries.)

☐ **Exercise 19. Looking at grammar.** (Chart 10-5)
Complete the sentences by changing the active modals to passive.

1. Someone must send this letter immediately.
   This letter ___*must be sent*___ immediately.

2. People should plant tomatoes in the spring.
   Tomatoes _____ in the spring.

3. People cannot control the weather.
   The weather _____.

4. Someone had to fix our car before we left for Chicago.
   Our car _____ before we left for Chicago.

5. People can reach me on my cell at 555-3815.
   I _____ on my cell at 555-3815.

6. Someone ought to wash these dirty dishes soon.

These dirty dishes _____ soon.

7. People may cook carrots or eat them raw.

Carrots _____ or _____ raw.

8. Be careful! If that email file has a virus, it could destroy your reports.

Your reports _____ if that email file has a virus.

9. You must keep medicine out of the reach of children.

Medicine _____ out of the reach of children.

□ **Exercise 20. Reading.** (Charts 10-1 → 10-5)
Part I. Read the questions and then the passage about jeans.

Are you wearing jeans right now, or do you have a pair at home?
If so, who were they made by?

The Origin of Jeans

Around the world, a very popular pant for men, women, and children is jeans. Did you know that jeans were created more than 100 years ago? They were invented by Levi Strauss during the California Gold Rush.

In 1853, Levi Strauss, a 24-year-old immigrant from Germany, traveled from New York to San Francisco. His brother was the owner of a store in New York and wanted to open another one in San Francisco. When Strauss arrived, a gold miner* asked him what he had to sell. Levi said he had strong canvas for tents and wagon covers. The miner told him he really needed strong pants because he couldn't find any that lasted very long.

So Levi Strauss took the canvas and designed a pair of overall pants. The miners liked them except that they were rough on the skin. Strauss exchanged the canvas for a cotton cloth from France called *serge de Nimes*. Later, the fabric was called "denim" and the pants were given the nickname "blue jeans."

Eventually, Levi Strauss & Company was formed. Strauss and tailor David Jacobs began putting rivets** in pants to make them stronger. In 1936, a red tab was added to the rear pocket. This was done so "Levis" could be more easily identified. Nowadays the company is very well known, and for many people, all jeans are known as Levis.

Part II. Answer the questions in complete sentences.

1. Who was Levi Strauss?
2. Why did Strauss go to California?
3. Who were jeans first created for?
4. What is denim?
5. What two changes were later made to jeans?
6. Why were rivets put in jeans?
7. Why was a red tab added to the rear pocket?
8. Many people have a different name for blue jeans. What is it?

---

*gold miner = a person who digs for gold

**rivet = a very strong pin to hold the seams of clothing together

Do you know this trivia?★ Complete the sentences with words from the list.

China	monkeys	sand	spiders
Mongolia	Nepal	small spaces	whales

1. Glass is composed mainly of _____.

2. Dolphins are related to _____.

3. The Gobi Desert is located in two countries: _____ and

   _____.

4. People with claustrophobia are frightened by _____.

10-6 Using Past Participles as Adjectives (Non-Progressive Passive)

	be	+	*adjective*	**Be** can be followed by an adjective, as in (a)–(c). The adjective describes or gives information about the subject of the sentence.
(a) Paul	*is*		*young.*	
(b) Paul	*is*		*tall.*	
(c) Paul	*is*		*hungry.*	
	be	+	*past participle*	**Be** can be followed by a past participle (the passive form), as in (d)–(f). The past participle is often like an adjective. The past participle describes or gives information about the subject of the sentence. Past participles are used as adjectives in many common, everyday expressions.
(d) Paul	*is*		*married.*	
(e) Paul	*is*		*tired.*	
(f) Paul	*is*		*frightened.*	

(g) Paul *is married **to** Susan.*	Often the past participles in these expressions are followed by particular prepositions + an object. For example:
(h) Paul *was excited **about** the game.*	In (g): **married** is followed by **to** (+ *an object*)
(i) Paul *will be prepared **for** the exam.*	In (h): **excited** is followed by **about** (+ *an object*)
	In (i): **prepared** is followed by **for** (+ *an object*)

Some Common Expressions with *Be* + Past Participle

be acquainted (*with*)	be excited (*about*)	be opposed (*to*)
be bored (*with, by*)	be exhausted (*from*)	be pleased (*with*)
be broken	be finished (*with*)	be prepared (*for*)
be closed	be frightened (*of, by, about*)	be qualified (*for*)
be composed of	be gone (*from*)	be related (*to*)
be crowded (*with*)	be hurt	be satisfied (*with*)
be devoted (*to*)	be interested (*in*)	be scared (*of, by*)
be disappointed (*in, with*)	be involved (*in, with*)	be shut
be divorced (*from*)	be located in / south of / etc.	be spoiled
be done (*with*)	be lost	be terrified (*of, by*)
be drunk (*on*)	be made of	be tired (*of, from*)★
be engaged (*to*)	be married (*to*)	be worried (*about*)

★I'm **tired** *of* the cold weather. = *I've had enough cold weather. I want the weather to get warm.*
I'm **tired** *from* working hard all day. = *I'm tired because I worked hard all day.*

★See *Trivia Answers*, p. 421.

❑ **Exercise 22. Looking at grammar.** (Chart 10-6)
Choose all the correct completions.

1. Roger is disappointed with _____.
   (a.) his job   b. in the morning   (c.) his son's grades

2. Are you related to _____?
   a. the Browns   b. math and science   c. me

3. Finally! We are done with _____.
   a. finished   b. our chores   c. our errands

4. My boss was pleased with _____.
   a. my report   b. thank you   c. the new contract

5. The baby birds are gone from _____.
   a. away   b. their nest   c. yesterday

6. Taka and JoAnne are bored with _____.
   a. their work   b. this movie   c. their marriage

7. Are you tired of _____?
   a. work   b. asleep   c. the news

❑ **Exercise 23. Looking at grammar.** (Chart 10-6)
Complete each sentence with an appropriate preposition.

Nervous Nick is . . .

1. worried _____ almost everything in life.

2. frightened _____ being around people.

3. also scared _____ snakes, lizards, and dogs.

4. terrified _____ going outside and seeing a dog.

5. exhausted _____ worrying so much.

Steady Steve is . . .

6. excited _____ waking up every morning.

7. pleased _____ his job.

8. interested _____ having a good time.

9. involved _____ many community activities.

10. satisfied _____ just about everything in his life.

Exercise 24. Looking at grammar. (Chart 10-6)

Complete the sentences with the present form of the given verbs. Note the **boldface** prepositions that follow them.

compose	interest	oppose	satisfy
finish	marry	prepare	✓scare

1. Most children __are scared__ **of** loud noises.

2. Jane _____ **in** ecology.

3. Don't clear the table yet. I _____ not _____ **with** my meal.

4. I _____ **with** my progress in English.

5. Tony _____ **to** Sonia. They have a happy marriage.

6. Roberta's parents _____ **to** her marriage. They don't like her fiancé.

7. The test is tomorrow. _____ you _____ **for** it?

8. A digital picture _____ **of** thousands of tiny dots called pixels.

Exercise 25. Looking at grammar. (Chart 10-6)

Complete each sentence with an appropriate preposition.

1. Because of the sale, the mall was crowded _____ shoppers.

2. Do you think you are qualified _____ that job?

3. Mr. Ahmad loves his family very much. He is devoted _____ them.

4. My sister is married _____ a law student.

5. I'll be finished _____ my work in another minute or two.

6. The workers are opposed _____ the new health-care plan.

7. Are you acquainted _____ this writer? I can't put her books down!*

8. Janet doesn't take good care of herself. I'm worried _____ her health.

---

can't put a book down = can't stop reading a book because it's so exciting/interesting

❑ **Exercise 26. Listening.** (Chart 10-6)

Listen to the sentences and write the prepositions you hear.

Example: You will hear: Linda loves her grandchildren. She is devoted to them.
        You will write: ___to___

1. _____   5. _____

2. _____   6. _____

3. _____   7. _____

4. _____   8. _____

❑ **Exercise 27. Looking at grammar.** (Chart 10-6)

Complete the sentences with expressions in the list. Use the present and add prepositions as necessary.

be acquainted	be exhausted	be qualified
be composed	be located	be spoiled
be crowded	be made	✓be worried
be disappointed		

1. Dennis isn't doing well in school this semester. He ___is worried about___ his grades.

2. My shirt _____ cotton.

3. I live in a three-room apartment with six other people. Our apartment _____

   _____.

4. Vietnam _____ Southeast Asia.

5. I'm going to go straight to bed tonight. It's been a hard day. I _____.

6. The kids _____. I had promised to take them to the

   beach today, but now we can't go because it's raining.

7. This milk doesn't taste right. I think it _____. I'm not going to

   drink it.

8. Water _____ hydrogen and oxygen.

9. According to the job description, an applicant must have a master's degree and at least five

   years of teaching experience. Unfortunately, I _____ not _____

   that job.

10. A: Have you ever met Mrs. Novinsky?

    B: No, I _____ not _____ her.

□ **Exercise 28. Listening.** (Chart 10-6)

Complete the sentences with the words you hear.

Example: You will hear: My earrings are made of gold.

You will write: *are made of*

1. This fruit _____. I think I'd better throw it out.

2. When we got to the post office, it _____.

3. Oxford University _____ Oxford, England.

4. Haley doesn't like to ride in elevators. She's _____ small spaces.

5. What's the matter? _____ you _____?

6. Excuse me. Could you please tell me how to get to the bus station from here?

   I _____.

7. Your name is Tom Hood? _____ you _____ Mary Hood?

8. Where's my wallet? It's _____! Did someone take it?

9. Oh, no! Look at my sunglasses. I sat on them and now they _____.

10. It's starting to rain. _____ all of the windows _____?

□ **Exercise 29. Warm-up.** (Chart 10-7)

Match three of the sentences with the pictures. One sentence does not match either picture.

Picture A

Picture B

1. The shark is terrifying. _____
2. The shark is terrified. _____
3. The swimmer is terrifying. _____
4. The swimmer is terrified. _____

The Passive   **275**

10-7 Participial Adjectives: -ed vs. -ing

Art **interests** me. (a) I am *interested* in art. INCORRECT: *I am interesting in art.* (b) Art is *interesting*. INCORRECT: *Art is interested.* The news **surprised** Kate. (c) Kate was *surprised*. (d) The news was *surprising*.	The past participle (**-ed**)* and the present participle (**-ing**) can be used as adjectives. In (a): The past participle (***interested***) describes how a person feels. In (b): The present participle (***interesting***) describes the **cause** of the feeling. The cause of the interest is art. In (c): ***surprised*** describes how Kate felt. The past participle carries a passive meaning: *Kate was surprised **by the news**.* In (d): ***the news*** was the cause of the surprise.
(e) Did you hear the *surprising news*? (f) Roberto fixed the *broken window*.	Like other adjectives, participial adjectives may follow **be**, as in examples (a) through (d), or they may come in front of nouns, as in (e) and (f).

*The past participle of regular verbs ends in **-ed**. For verbs that have irregular forms, see the inside back cover.

☐ **Exercise 30. Looking at grammar.** (Chart 10-7)
Complete the sentences with the correct word: *girl, man,* or *roller coaster.*

1. The _____ is frightened.

2. The _____ is frightening.

3. The _____ is excited.

4. The _____ is exciting.

5. The _____ is thrilling.

6. The _____ is delighted.

☐ **Exercise 31. Listening.** (Chart 10-7)
Listen to the statements and choose the words you hear.

Example: You will hear: It was a frightening experience.

You will choose: frighten   (frightening)   frightened

1. bore	boring	bored
2. shock	shocking	shocked
3. confuse	confusing	confused
4. embarrass	embarrassing	embarrassed
5. surprise	surprising	surprised
6. scare	scary*	scared

*The adjective ending is **-y**, not **-ing**.

□ **Exercise 32. Looking at grammar.** (Chart 10-7)
Complete the sentences with the **-ed** or **-ing** form of the verbs in *italics*.

1. Talal's classes *interest* him.

   a. Talal's classes are ___*interesting*___ .

   b. Talal is an ___*interested*___ student.

2. Emily is going to Australia. The idea of going on this trip *excites* her.

   a. Emily is _____ about going on this trip.

   b. She thinks it is going to be an _____ trip.

3. I like to study sea life. The subject of marine biology *fascinates* me.

   a. Marine biology is a _____ subject.

   b. I'm _____ by marine biology.

4. Mike heard some bad news. The bad news *depressed* him.

   a. Mike is very sad. In fact, he is _____ .

   b. The news made Mike feel very sad. The news was _____ .

5. The exploration of space *interests* me.

   a. I'm _____ in the exploration of space.

   b. The exploration of space is _____ to me.

□ **Exercise 33. Listening.** (Chart 10-7)
Listen to each sentence and circle the word you hear.

SITUATION: Julie was walking along the edge of the fountain outside her office building. She was with her co-worker and friend Paul. Suddenly she lost her balance and accidentally fell into the water.

1.	embarrassed	embarrassing	6.	surprised	surprising
2.	embarrassed	embarrassing	7.	upset★	upsetting
3.	shocked	shocking	8.	depressed	depressing
4.	shocked	shocking	9.	interested	interesting
5.	surprised	surprising	10.	interested	interesting

❑ **Exercise 34. Warm-up.** (Chart 10-8)
Are any of these statements true for you? Circle *yes* or *no*.

Right now . . .

1. I am getting tired. yes no
2. I am getting hungry. yes no
3. I am getting confused. yes no

10-8 *Get* + Adjective; *Get* + Past Participle

Get + **Adjective**	
(a) I *am getting hungry*. Let's eat. (b) Eric *got nervous* before the job interview.	*Get* can be followed by an adjective. *Get* gives the idea of change — the idea of becoming, beginning to be, growing to be. In (a): *I'm getting hungry.* = I wasn't hungry before, but now I'm beginning to be hungry.
Get + **Past Participle**	
(c) I *'m getting tired*. Let's stop working. (d) Steve and Rita *got married* last month.	Sometimes *get* is followed by a past participle. The past participle after *get* is like an adjective; it describes the subject of the sentence.

Get + **Adjective**			*Get* + **Past Participle**		
get angry	get dry	get quiet	get acquainted	get drunk	get involved
get bald	get fat	get rich	get arrested	get engaged	get killed
get big	get full	get serious	get bored	get excited	get lost
get busy	get hot	get sick	get confused	get finished	get married
get close	get hungry	get sleepy	get crowded	get frightened	get scared
get cold	get interested	get thirsty	get divorced	get hurt	get sunburned
get dark	get late	get well	get done	get interested	get tired
get dirty	get nervous	get wet	get dressed	get invited	get worried
get dizzy	get old				

★There is no *-ed* ending.

□ **Exercise 35. Looking at grammar.** (Chart 10-8)
Complete the sentences with the words in the list.

bald	dirty	hurt	lost	rich
busy	✓full	late	nervous	serious

1. This food is delicious, but I can't eat any more. I'm getting ___full___.

2. This work has to be done before we leave. We'd better get _____ and stop wasting time.

3. I didn't understand Mariam's directions very well, so on the way to her house last night I got _____. I couldn't find her house.

4. It's hard to work on a car and stay clean. Paul's clothes always get _____ from all the grease and oil.

5. Tim doesn't like to fly. As soon as he sits down, his heart starts to beat quickly. He gets really _____.

6. We'd better go home. It's getting _____, and you have school tomorrow.

7. Simon wants to get _____, but he doesn't want to work. That's not very realistic.

8. If you plan to go to medical school, you need to get _____ about the time and money involved and start planning now.

9. Mr. Andersen is losing some of his hair. He's slowly getting _____.

10. Was the accident serious? Did anyone get _____?

□ **Exercise 36. Let's talk: interview.** (Chart 10-8)
Interview your classmates. Share some of their answers with the class.

1. Have you ever gotten hurt? What happened?
2. Have you ever gotten lost? What happened?
3. When was the last time you got dizzy?
4. How long does it take you to get dressed in the morning?
5. In general, do you get sleepy during the day? When?
6. Do you ever get hungry in the middle of the night? What do you do?
7. Have you ever gotten involved with a charity? Which one?

□ **Exercise 37. Listening.** (Chart 10-8)

Listen to the sentences and complete them with any adjectives that make sense.

Example: You will hear: This towel is soaking wet. Please hang it up so it will get . . .
     You will write: ___dry___

1. _____   4. _____

2. _____   5. _____

3. _____   6. _____

□ **Exercise 38. Looking at grammar.** (Chart 10-8)

Complete the sentences with appropriate forms of **get** and the words in the list.

angry	dressed	kill	tired
cold	dry	lost	well
crowd	hungry	marry	worry
dark	involve	✓sunburn	

1. When I stayed out in the sun too long yesterday, I ___got sunburned___.

2. If you're sick, stay home and take care of yourself. You won't _____ if you don't take care of yourself.

3. Alima and Hasan are engaged. They are going to _____ a year from now.

4. Sarah doesn't eat breakfast, so she always _____ by ten or ten-thirty.

5. In the winter, the sun sets early. It _____ outside by six or even earlier.

6. Put these towels back in the dryer. They didn't _____ the first time.

7. Let's stop working for a while. I'm _____. I need a break.

8. Anastasia has to move out of her apartment next week, and she hasn't found a new place to live. She's _____.

9. Toshiro was in a terrible car wreck and almost _____. He's lucky to be alive.

10. The temperature is dropping. Brrr! I'm _____. Can I borrow your sweater?

11. Sorry we're late. We took a wrong turn and _____.

12. Good restaurants _____ around dinner time. It's hard to find a seat because there are so many people.

13. Calm down! Take it easy! You shouldn't _____ so _____. It's not good for your blood pressure.

14. I left when Ellen and Joe began to argue. I never _____ in other people's quarrels.

15. Sam is wearing one brown sock and one blue sock today. He _____ in a hurry this morning and didn't pay attention to the color of his socks.

❑ **Exercise 39. Reading.** (Chart 10-8)
Read the passage and the statements that follow it. Circle "T" for true and "F" for false.

A Blended Family

Lisa and Thomas live in a blended family. They are not related to each other, but they are brother and sister. Actually, they are stepbrother and stepsister. This is how they came to be in the same family.

Lisa's mother got divorced when Lisa was a baby. Thomas' father was a widower. His wife had died seven years earlier. Lisa and Thomas' parents met five years ago at a going-away party for a friend. After a year of dating, they got engaged and a year later, they got married. Lisa and Thomas are about the same age and get along well. Theirs is a happy, blended family.

1. Lisa's mother got married. Then she got divorced. Then she got remarried.   T   F

2. Thomas' father got married, and then he got divorced. After he got divorced, he got engaged, and then he got remarried.   T   F

3. Lisa and Thomas became stepsister and stepbrother when their parents got remarried.   T   F

❑ **Exercise 40. Warm-up.** (Chart 10-9)
Circle the words in *italics* that make these sentences true for you.

1. I am *used to, not used to* speaking English with native speakers.

2. I am *accustomed to, not accustomed to* speaking English without translating from my language.

3. I am *getting used to, not getting used to* English slang.

4. I am *getting accustomed to, not getting accustomed to* reading English without a dictionary.

10-9 Using *Be Used/Accustomed To* and *Get Used/Accustomed To*

(a) I **am used to** hot weather. (b) I **am accustomed to** hot weather.	Examples (a) and (b) have the same meaning: "Living in a hot climate is usual and normal for me. I'm familiar with what it is like to live in a hot climate. Hot weather isn't strange or different to me."
(c) I *am used **to living*** in a hot climate. (d) I *am accustomed **to living*** in a hot climate.	Notice in (c) and (d): *to* (a preposition) is followed by the *-ing* form of a verb (a gerund).
(e) I just moved from Florida to Alaska. I have never lived in a cold climate before, but I **am getting used to** (**accustomed to**) the cold weather here.	In (e): *I'm getting used to/accustomed to* = something is beginning to seem usual and normal to me.

❑ **Exercise 41. Looking at grammar.** (Chart 10-9)

Part I. Complete the sentences with *be used to,* affirmative or negative.

1. Juan is from Mexico. He ___is used to___ hot weather. He ___isn't used to___ cold weather.

2. Alice was born and raised in Chicago. She _____ living in a big city.

3. My hometown is New York City, but this year I'm going to school in a town with a population of 10,000. I _____ living in a small town. I _____ living in a big city.

4. We do a lot of exercises in class. We _____ doing exercises.

Part II. Complete the sentences with *be accustomed to,* affirmative or negative.

5. Spiro recently moved to Hong Kong from Greece. He ___is accustomed to___ eating Greek food. He ___isn't accustomed to___ eating Chinese food.

6. I always get up around 6:00 A.M. I _____ getting up early. I _____ sleeping late.

7. Our teacher always gives us a lot of homework. We _____ having a lot of homework every day.

8. Young schoolchildren rarely take multiple-choice tests. They _____ taking that kind of test.

❑ **Exercise 42. Listening and speaking.** (Chart 10-9)

Part I. Complete the questions with the words you hear.

Example: You will hear: What time are you accustomed to getting up?
You will write: ___are you accustomed to___

1. What _____ doing in the evenings?

2. What time _____ going to bed?

3. What _____ having for breakfast?

4. _____ living in this area?

5. Do you live with someone or do you live alone? _____ that?

6. _____ speaking English every day?

7. What _____ doing on weekends?

8. What do you think about the weather here? _____ it?

Part II. Work with a partner. Take turns asking and answering the questions in Part I.

❑ **Exercise 43. Let's talk: interview.** (Chart 10-9)
Ask your classmates questions with **be used to/accustomed to**.

Example: buy \ frozen food
→ *Are you used to / accustomed to buying frozen food?*

1. get up \ early
2. sleep \ late
3. eat \ breakfast
4. skip \ lunch
5. eat \ a late dinner

6. drink \ coffee in the morning
7. have \ dessert at night
8. live \ in a big city
9. live \ in a small town
10. pay \ for all your expenses

❑ **Exercise 44. Let's talk.** (Chart 10-9)
Work in small groups. Discuss one or more of the given topics. Make a list of your answers. Share some of them with the class.

Topics:
1. Junko is going to leave her parents' house next week. She is going to move in with two of her cousins who work in the city. Junko will be away from her home for the first time in her life. What is she going to have to get accustomed to?

2. Think of a time you traveled in or lived in a foreign country. What weren't you used to? What did you get used to? What didn't you ever get used to?

3. Think of the first day of a job you have had. What weren't you used to? What did you get used to?

❑ **Exercise 45. Warm-up.** (Chart 10-10)
Complete the sentences about food preferences. Make statements that are true for you.

1. There are some foods I liked when I was younger, but now I don't eat them. I used to eat

_____, but now I don't.

2. There are some foods I didn't like when I first tried them, but now they're okay. For

example, the first time I ate _____, I didn't like it, but now I'm

used to eating them.

10-10 Used To vs. Be Used To

(a) I *used to live* in Chicago, but now I live in Tokyo. INCORRECT: *I used to living in Chicago.* INCORRECT: *I am used to live in a big city.*	In (a): **Used to** expresses the habitual past (see Chart 2-8, p. 53). It is followed by the **simple form of a verb.**
(b) I *am used to living* in a big city.	In (b): **be used to** is followed by the **-ing form of a verb** (a gerund).*

*NOTE: In both **used to** (habitual past) and **be used to**, the "d" is not pronounced.

❑ **Exercise 46. Looking at grammar.** (Chart 10-10)
Complete the sentences with an appropriate form of **be**. If no form of **be** is necessary, use Ø.

1. I have lived in Malaysia for a long time. I ___*am*___ used to warm weather.

2. I ___Ø___ used to live in Portugal, but now I live in Spain.

3. I _____ used to sitting at this desk. I sit here every day.

4. I _____ used to sit in the back of the classroom, but now I prefer to sit in the front row.

5. When I was a child, I _____ used to play games with my friends in a big field near my house after school every day.

6. It's hard for my kids to stay inside on a cold, rainy day. They _____ used to playing outside in the big field near our house. They play there almost every day.

7. A teacher _____ used to answering questions. Students, especially good students, always have a lot of questions.

8. People _____ used to believe the world was flat.

❑ **Exercise 47. Looking at grammar.** (Chart 10-10)
Complete the sentences with **used to/be used to** and the correct form of the verb in parentheses.

1. Nick stays up later now than he did when he was in high school. He (*go*) ___used to go___ to bed at ten, but now he rarely gets to bed before midnight.

2. I got used to going to bed late when I was in college, but now I have a job and I need my sleep. These days I (*go*) ___am used to going___ to bed around ten-thirty.

3. I am a vegetarian. I (*eat*) _____ meat, but now I eat only meatless meals.

4. Ms. Wu has had a vegetable garden all her life. She (*grow*) _____ her own vegetables.

5. Oscar has lived in Brazil for ten years. He (*eat*) _____
Brazilian food. It's his favorite.

6. Georgio moved to Germany to open his own restaurant. He (*have*) _____
_____ a small bakery in Italy.

7. I have taken the bus to work every day for the past five years. I (*take*) _____
_____ the bus.

8. Juanita travels by train on company business. She (*go*) _____
by plane, but now it's too expensive.

□ **Exercise 48. Warm-up.** (Chart 10-11)
Complete the sentences about airline passengers.

1. Before getting on the plane, passengers are expected to _____.

2. After boarding the plane, passengers are supposed to _____.

3. During landing, passengers are not supposed to _____.

10-11 Using *Be Supposed To*

(a) Mike *is supposed to call* me tomorrow. (IDEA: I expect Mike to call me tomorrow.) (b) We *are supposed to write* a composition. (IDEA: The teacher expects us to write a composition.)	*Be supposed to* is used to talk about an activity or event that is expected to occur. In (a): The idea of *is supposed to* is that Mike is expected (by me) to call me. I asked him to call me. He promised to call me. I expect him to call me.
(c) Alice *was supposed to be* home at ten, but she didn't get in until midnight. (IDEA: Someone expected Alice to be home at ten.)	In the past form, *be supposed to* often expresses the idea that an expected event did not occur, as in (c).

□ **Exercise 49. Looking at grammar.** (Chart 10-11)
Make a sentence with a similar meaning to the given sentence. Use *be supposed to*.

1. The teacher expects us to be on time for class.
   → *We are supposed to be on time for class.*

2. People expect the weather to be cold tomorrow.

3. People expect the plane to arrive at 6:00.

4. My boss expects me to work late tonight.

5. I expected the mail to come an hour ago, but it didn't.

❑ **Exercise 50. Let's talk.** (Chart 10-11)
Summarize each conversation with a statement. Use **be supposed to**. Work in pairs, in small groups, or as a class.

1. TOM'S BOSS: Mail this package.
   TOM: Yes, sir.

   → *Tom is supposed to mail a package.*

2. LENA: Call me at nine.
   ANN: Okay.

3. MS. MARTINEZ: Please make your bed before you go to school.
   JOHNNY: Okay, Mom.

4. PROF. THOMPSON: Read the test directions carefully and raise your hand if you have any questions.
   STUDENTS: (*no response*)

5. DR. KEMPER: You should take one pill every eight hours.
   PATIENT: Right. Anything else?
   DR. KEMPER: Drink plenty of fluids.

❑ **Exercise 51. Listening.** (Chart 10-11)
Listen to the statements with **be supposed to**. Choose "T" for true and "F" for false. Notice that **to** in **be supposed to** sounds like "ta."

Example: You will hear: Visitors at a museum are not supposed to touch the art.
   You will choose: (T)   F

1. T F	5. T F
2. T F	6. T F
3. T F	7. T F
4. T F	8. T F

❑ **Exercise 52. Reading, grammar, and listening.** (Chapter 10)
Part I. Answer the questions and then read the passage on zoos.

Have you visited a zoo recently?
What was your opinion of it?
Were the animals well-taken care of?
Did they live in natural settings or in cages?

Zoos

Zoos are common around the world. The first zoo was established around 3,500 years ago by an Egyptian queen for her enjoyment. Five hundred years later, a Chinese emperor established a huge zoo to show his power and wealth. Later, zoos were established for the purpose of studying animals.

Zoos were supposed to take good care of animals, but some of the early ones were dark holes or dirty cages. At that time, people became disgusted with the poor care the animals were given. Later, these early zoos were replaced by scientific institutions. Animals were studied and kept in better conditions there. These research centers became the first modern zoos.

Because zoos want to treat animals well and encourage breeding, animals today are put in large, natural settings instead of small cages. They are fed a healthy diet and are watched carefully for any signs of disease. Most zoos have specially trained veterinarians and a hospital for their animals. Today, animals in these zoos are treated well, and zoo breeding programs have saved many different types of animals.

Part II. Circle all the grammatically correct statements.

1. a. The first zoo was established around 3,500 years ago.
   b. The first zoo established around 3,500 years ago.
   c. An Egyptian queen established the first zoo.

2. a. Zoos supposed to take good care of animals.
   b. Zoos were supposed to take good care of animals.
   c. Zoos were suppose to take good care of animals.

3. a. The animals was poorly cared for in some of the early zoos.
   b. The animals were poorly cared for in some of the early zoos.
   c. The early zoos didn't take good care of the animals.

4. a. Today, animals are kept in more natural settings.
   b. Today, zoos keep animals in more natural settings.
   c. Today, more natural settings are provided for animals.

5. a. Nowadays, animals are treated better in zoos than before.
   b. Nowadays, animals are taken better care of in zoos than before.
   c. Nowadays, animals take care of in zoos than before.

Part III. Listen to the passage. Complete the sentences with the verbs you hear and then answer the questions.

Zoos

Zoos are common around the world. The first zoo ___was___ established around 3,500
                                            1
years ago by an Egyptian queen for her enjoyment. Five hundred years later, a Chinese

emperor _____ a huge zoo to show his power and wealth. Later, zoos
                    2

_____ for the purpose of studying animals.
                    3

    Zoos _____ take good care of animals, but some of
                        4

the early ones were dark holes or dirty cages. At that time, people _____
                                                                                5

disgusted with the poor care the animals _____. Later, these early
                                                            6

zoos _____ replaced by scientific institutions. Animals _____
            7   8

and _____ in better conditions there. These research centers became the first
        9

modern zoos.

Because zoos want to treat animals well and encourage breeding, animals today

_____ in large, natural settings instead of small cages. They
　　　　　10

_____ a healthy diet and _____ carefully for any signs of
　　　　　11　　　　　　　　　　　　　　　　　　　　12

disease. Most zoos _____ specially trained veterinarians and a hospital for their
　　　　　　　　　　　　13

animals. Today, animals in these zoos _____ well, and zoo breeding
　　　　　　　　　　　　　　　　　　　　　　14

programs _____ many different types of animals.
　　　　　　　　15

1. Why was the first zoo established?
2. What were some of the early zoos like?
3. What was the purpose of the first modern zoos?
4. What are zoos doing to encourage breeding?
5. Why do zoos want to encourage breeding?

❑ **Exercise 53. Check your knowledge.** (Chapter 10)
Edit the sentences.

1. I ~~am~~ agree with him.

2. Something was happened.

3. This pen is belong to me.

4. I'm interesting in that subject.

5. He is marry with my cousin.

6. Mary's dog was died last week.

7. Were you surprise when you heard the news?

8. When I went downtown, I am get lost.

9. The bus was arrived ten minutes late.

10. We're not suppose to have pets in our apartment.

Exercise 54. Reading and writing. (Chapter 10)
Part I. Read the passage and <u>underline</u> the passive verbs.

My Favorite Holiday

(1) New Year's is the most important holiday of the yea〉
<u>celebrated</u> for fifteen days, but my favorite day is the first c

(2) The celebration actually begins at midnight. Firewc
filled with people. Neighbors and friends greet each other
the year. The next morning, gifts are exchanged. Childrer
red envelopes because red is the color for good luck. Wher
favorite part of the holiday.

(3) On New Year's Day, everyone wears new clothes. T〉
the holiday. People are very polite to each other. It is considered wrong to yell, lie, or use bad
language on the first day of the year. It is a custom for younger generations to visit their elders.
They wish them good health and a long life.

Part II. Choose a holiday you like. Describe the activities on this day. What do you do in the
morning? afternoon? evening? Which activities do you enjoy the most? Make some of your
sentences passive.

Chapter 11

Count/Noncount Nouns and Articles

☐ **Exercise 1. Warm-up.** (Chart 11-1)
Check (✓) all the items you have with you right now. Do you know why some nouns have **a** before them and others have **an?**

1. _____ **a** pen
2. _____ **an** eraser
3. _____ **a** notebook
4. _____ **an** umbrella
5. _____ **an** interesting book
6. _____ **a** university map

11-1 *A* vs. *An*

(a) I have *a pencil*. (b) I live in *an apartment*. (c) I have *a small apartment*. (d) I live in *an old building*.	*A* and *an* are used in front of a singular noun (e.g., *pencil, apartment*). They mean "one." If a singular noun is modified by an adjective (e.g., *small, old*), *a* or *an* comes in front of the adjective, as in (c) and (d). *A* is used in front of words that begin with a consonant (*b, c, d, f, g,* etc.): *a boy, a bad day, a cat, a cute baby.* *An* is used in front of words that begin with the vowels *a, e, i,* and *o*: *an apartment, an angry man, an elephant, an empty room,* etc.

(e) I have *an umbrella*.
(f) I saw *an ugly picture*.
(g) I attend *a university*.
(h) I had *a unique experience*.
	For words that begin with the letter *u*:
	  (1) *An* is used if the *u* is a vowel sound, as in *an umbrella, an uncle, an unusual day.*
	  (2) *A* is used if the *u* is a consonant sound, as in *a university, a unit, a usual event.*

(i) He will arrive in *an hour*.
(j) New Year's Day is *a holiday*.
	For words that begin with the letter *h*:
	  (1) *An* is used if the *h* is silent: *an hour, an honor, an honest person.*
	  (2) *A* is used if the *h* is pronounced: *a holiday, a hotel, a high grade.*

❏ **Exercise 2. Looking at grammar.** (Chart 11-1)
Add *a* or *an* to these words.

1. _a_ mistake
2. ____ abbreviation
3. ____ dream
4. ____ interesting dream
5. ____ empty box
6. ____ box
7. ____ uniform
8. ____ email
9. ____ untrue story

10. ____ urgent message
11. ____ universal problem
12. ____ unhappy child
13. ____ hour or two
14. ____ hole in the ground
15. ____ hill
16. ____ handsome man
17. ____ honest man
18. ____ honor

❏ **Exercise 3. Listening.** (Chart 11-1)
Listen to the sentences. Decide if you hear *a*, *an*, or *Ø* (no article).

Example: You will hear: I have a bad toothache.
You will choose: ⓐ   an   Ø

1. a   an   Ø
2. a   an   Ø
3. a   an   Ø
4. a   an   Ø
5. a   an   Ø

6. a   an   Ø
7. a   an   Ø
8. a   an   Ø
9. a   an   Ø
10. a   an   Ø

❏ **Exercise 4. Warm-up.** (Chart 11-2)
Circle all the correct completions.

1. I need one ____ .
   a. chair   b. chairs

2. There are two ____ in the room.
   a. chairs   b. furniture

3. I found some ____ in the storage room.
   a. chairs   b. furniture

4. I found ____ in the storage room.
   a. chairs   b. furniture

11-2 Count and Noncount Nouns

	Singular	Plural	
COUNT NOUN	*a* chair *one* chair	Ø chairs *two* chairs *some* chairs	A count noun: (1) can be counted with numbers: *one chair, two chairs, ten chairs, etc.* (2) can be preceded by **a/an** in the singular: *a chair.* (3) has a plural form ending in **-s** or **-es**: *chairs.**

NONCOUNT NOUN	Ø furniture
	some furniture
		Ø
		Ø
			A noncount noun:
			(1) cannot be counted with numbers.
			   INCORRECT: *one furniture*
			(2) is NOT immediately preceded by **a/an**.
			   INCORRECT: *a furniture*
			(3) does NOT have a plural form (no final **-s**).
			   INCORRECT: *furnitures*

*See Chart 1-5, p. 14, and Chart 6-1, p. 147, for the spelling and pronunciation of **-s/-es**.

❑ **Exercise 5. Looking at grammar.** (Chart 11-2)
Check (✓) the correct sentences. Correct the sentences with errors. Use *some* with the noncount nouns.

some furniture

one chair

two chairs

some chairs

1. __✓__ I bought one chair for my apartment.
2. _____ I bought ~~one~~ *some* furniture for my apartment.*
3. _____ I bought four chairs for my apartment.
4. _____ I bought four furnitures for my apartment.
5. _____ I bought a chair for my apartment.
6. _____ I bought a furniture for my apartment.
7. _____ I bought some chair for my apartment.
8. _____ I bought some furnitures for my apartment.

❑ **Exercise 6. Warm-up.** (Chart 11-3)
Write the words under the correct categories.

bracelets	ideas	letters	postcards	rings	suggestions

Advice	Mail	Jewelry
_____	_____	_____
_____	_____	_____

*CORRECT: *I bought **some furniture** for my apartment.* OR *I bought **furniture** for my apartment.* See Chart 11–8 for more information about the use of Ø and **some**.

11-3 Noncount Nouns

| Individual Parts → The Whole | | Noncount nouns usually refer to a whole group of things that is made up of many individual parts, a whole category made of different varieties. |
| (Count Nouns) (Noncount Nouns) | | |

(a) letters, postcards, bills, etc. → *mail*

(b) apples, bananas, oranges, etc. → *fruit*

(c) rings, bracelets, necklaces, etc. → *jewelry*

Noncount nouns usually refer to a whole group of things that is made up of many individual parts, a whole category made of different varieties.

For example, *furniture* is a noncount noun; it describes a whole category of things: *chairs, tables, beds, etc.*

chairs, tables, beds, etc. → **furniture**

Mail, fruit, and *jewelry* are other examples of noncount nouns that refer to a whole category made up of individual parts.

Some Common Noncount Nouns: Whole Groups Made up of Individual Parts

A. clothing	B. homework	E. grammar	G. corn
equipment	housework	slang	dirt
food	work	vocabulary	flour
fruit			hair
furniture	C. advice	F. Arabic	pepper
jewelry	information	Chinese	rice
mail		English	salt
money	D. history	German	sand
scenery	literature	Indonesian	sugar
stuff	music	Spanish	
traffic	poetry	Etc.	

❑ **Exercise 7. Looking at grammar.** (Charts 11-2 and 11-3)
Complete the sentences with *a/an* or *some*. Decide if the **boldface** nouns are count or noncount.

1. I often have ___some___ **fruit** for dessert.   count   (noncount)

2. I had ___a___ **banana** for dessert.   count   noncount

3. I got _____ **letter** today.   count   noncount

4. I got _____ **mail** today.   count   noncount

5. Anna wears _____ **ring** on her left hand.   count   noncount

6. Maria is wearing _____ **jewelry** today.   count   noncount

7. I have _____ **homework** to finish.   count   noncount

8. I have _____ **assignment** to finish.   count   noncount

9. I needed _____ **information**.   count   noncount

10. I asked _____ **question**.   count   noncount

❏ **Exercise 8. Grammar and speaking.** (Charts 11-2 and 11-3)
Add final *-s*/*-es* if possible. Otherwise, write **Ø**. Then decide if you agree or disagree with the statement. Discuss your answers.

1. I'm learning a lot of **grammar** _Ø_ this term. yes no

2. Count and noncount **noun** _s_ are easy. yes no

3. A good way to control **traffic** ____ is to charge people money
   to drive in the city. yes no

4. Electric **car** ____ will replace gas **car** ____. yes no

5. **Information** ____ from the Internet is usually reliable. yes no

6. **Fact** ____ are always true. yes no

7. Many **word** ____ in English are similar to those in my language. yes no

8. The best way to learn new **vocabulary** ____ is to memorize it. yes no

9. I enjoy singing karaoke **song** ____. yes no

10. I enjoy listening to classical **music** ____. yes no

11. I like to read good **literature** ____. yes no

12. I like to read mystery **novel** ____. yes no

13. **Beach** ____ are relaxing places to visit. yes no

14. Walking on **sand** ____ is good exercise for your legs. yes no

15. Parents usually have helpful **suggestion** ____ for their kids. yes no

16. Sometimes kids have helpful **advice** ____ for their parents. yes no

❏ **Exercise 9. Warm-up.** (Chart 11-4)
Complete the sentences with words from the list. Make sentences that are true for you.

beauty	health	milk	pollution	traffic
coffee	honesty	money	smog	violence
happiness	juice	noise	tea	water

1. During the day, I drink _____ or _____.

2. Two things I don't like about big cities are _____ and
   _____.

3. _____ is more important than _____.

11-4 More Noncount Nouns

(a) **Liquids**		**Solids and Semi-Solids**				**Gases**
coffee	soup	bread	meat	chalk	paper	air
milk	tea	butter	beef	glass	soap	pollution
oil	water	cheese	chicken	gold	toothpaste	smog
		ice	fish	iron	wood	smoke

(b) **Things That Occur in Nature**		
weather	darkness	thunder
rain	light	lightning
snow	sunshine	

(c) **Abstractions***					
beauty	fun	health	ignorance	luck	selfishness
courage	generosity	help	kindness	patience	time
experience	happiness	honesty	knowledge	progress	violence

*An abstraction is an idea. It has no physical form. A person cannot touch it.

❑ **Exercise 10. Looking at grammar.** (Charts 11-2 → 11-4)
Add final **-s/-es** if possible. Otherwise, write **Ø**. Choose verbs in parentheses as necessary.

1. I made some **mistake** _s_ on my algebra test.

2. In winter in Siberia, there ((is), are) **snow** _Ø_ on the ground.

3. Siberia has very cold **weather** _____ .

4. Be sure to give the new couple my best **wish** _____ .

5. I want to wish them good **luck** _____ .

6. **Silver** _____ (is, are) expensive. **Diamond** _____ (is, are) expensive too.

7. I admire Professor Yoo for her extensive **knowledge** _____ of organic farming methods.

8. Professor Yoo has a lot of good **idea** _____ and strong **opinion** _____ .

9. Teaching children to read requires **patience** _____ .

10. Doctors take care of **patient** _____ .

11. Mr. Fernandez's English is improving. He's making **progress** _____ .

12. Wood stoves are a source of **pollution** _____ in many cities.

❑ **Exercise 11. Listening.** (Charts 11-2 → 11-4)

Listen to the sentences. Add **-s** if the given nouns have plural endings. Otherwise, write **Ø**.

Example: You will hear: Watch out! There's ice on the sidewalk.
You will write: ice __Ø__

1. chalk____   6. storm_____

2. soap____   7. storm_____

3. suggestion_____   8. toothpaste____

4. suggestion_____   9. stuff_____

5. gold_____   10. equipment_____

❑ **Exercise 12. Let's talk.** (Chart 11-4)

Work in small groups. These common sayings use abstract nouns. Choose two sayings to explain to the class.

Example: Ignorance is bliss.
→ ***Ignorance*** *means you don't know about something.* ***Bliss*** *means happiness.*
This saying means that you are happier if you don't know about a problem.

1. Honesty is the best policy.   4. Knowledge is power.
2. Time is money.   5. Experience is the best teacher.
3. Laughter is the best medicine.

❑ **Exercise 13. Let's talk.** (Chart 11-4)

Complete the sentences. Give two to four answers for each item. Share your answers with a partner. See how many of your answers are the same. *Note:* Abstract nouns are usually noncount. To find out if a noun is count or noncount, check your dictionary or ask your teacher.

1. Qualities I admire in a person are . . . .
2. Bad qualities people can have are . . . .
3. Some of the most important things in life are . . . .
4. Certain bad conditions exist in the world. Some of them are . . . .

❑ **Exercise 14. Game.** (Charts 11-1 → 11-4)

Work in small teams. Imagine your team is at one of the given places. Make a list of the things you see. Share your team's list with the class. The team with the most complete and grammatically correct list wins.

Example: a teacher's office
→ *two windows*
→ *a lot of grammar books*
→ *office equipment — a computer, a printer, a photocopy machine*
→ *office supplies — a stapler, paper clips, pens, pencils, a ruler*
→ *some pictures*
etc.

Places:

a restaurant	an island
a museum	a hotel
a popular department store	an airport

❑ **Exercise 15. Warm-up.** (Chart 11-5)
Complete the sentences with **apples** or **fruit**.

1. I bought several _____ yesterday.

2. Do you eat a lot of _____?

3. Do you eat many _____?

4. Do you eat much _____?

5. I eat a few _____ every week.

6. I eat a little _____ for breakfast.

11-5 Using *Several, A Lot Of, Many/Much,* and *A Few/A Little*

	Count	Noncount	
(a)	*several* chairs	Ø	**Several** is used only with count nouns.
(b)	*a lot of* chairs	*a lot of* furniture	**A lot of** is used with both count and noncount nouns.
(c)	*many* chairs	*much* furniture	**Many** is used with count nouns. **Much** is used with noncount nouns.
(d)	*a few* chairs	*a little* furniture	**A few** is used with count nouns. **A little** is used with noncount nouns.

❑ **Exercise 16. Looking at grammar.** (Charts 11-2 and 11-5)
Check (✓) the correct sentences. Correct the sentences that have mistakes. One sentence has a spelling error.

some / Ø
1. _____ Jakob learned ~~several~~ new vocabulary.

2. __✓__ He learned several new words.

3. _____ Takashi learned a lot of new words.

4. _____ Sonia learned a lot of new vocabulary too.

5. _____ Lydia doesn't like learning too much new vocabulary in one day.

6. _____ She can't remember too much new words.

7. _____ Mr. Lee assigned a few vocabulary to his class.

8. _____ He assigned a few new words.

9. _____ He explained several new vocabulary.

10. _____ There is alot of new word at this level.

11. _____ There are a lot of new vocabulary at this level.

❑ **Exercise 17. Looking at grammar: pairwork.** (Charts 11-1 → 11-5)
Work with a partner. Take turns completing the questions with ***how many*** or ***how much.****
Make nouns plural as necessary.

1. How _____ does Mr. Miller have?
   a. son   → *many sons*   d. car
   b. child → *many children*   e. stuff
   c. work   → *much work*   f. experience

2. How _____ did you buy?
   a. fruit   d. tomato
   b. vegetable   e. orange
   c. banana   f. food

3. How _____ did you have?
   a. fun   d. information
   b. help   e. fact
   c. time   f. money

❑ **Exercise 18. Let's talk: interview.** (Chart 11-5)
Interview your classmates. Begin your questions with ***How much*** or ***How many.*** Share
some of your answers with the class.

How much/How many . . .
1. pages does this book have?
2. coffee do you drink every day?
3. cups of tea do you drink every day?
4. homework do you have to do tonight?
5. assignments have you had this week?
6. provinces does Canada have?
7. countries does Africa have?
8. snow does this area get in the winter?

***Much** and **many** are more commonly used in questions than in affirmative statements.

☐ **Exercise 19. Looking at grammar.** (Charts 11-1 → 11-5)
Complete the sentences with *a few* or *a little* and the given noun. Use the plural form of the noun as necessary.

1. music   I feel like listening to ___*a little music*___ tonight.

2. song   We sang ___*a few songs*___ at the party.

3. help   Do you need _____ with that?

4. pepper   My grandfather doesn't use salt, but he always puts
              _____ on his eggs.

5. thing   I need to pick up _____ at the store on my way
              home from work tonight.

6. apple   I bought _____ at the store.★

7. fruit   I bought _____ at the store.

8. advice   I need _____.

9. money   If I accept that job, I'll make _____ more _____.

10. friend   _____ came by last night to visit us.

11. rain   It looks like we might get _____ today. I
              think I'll take my umbrella with me.

12. French   I can speak _____, but I don't know any
              Italian at all.

13. hour   Ron's plane will arrive in _____ more _____.

☐ **Exercise 20. Warm-up.** (Chart 11-6)
Match the sentences to the pictures.

  Picture A   Picture B   Picture C

1. Do you need one glass or two?
2. Your glasses fit nicely.
3. A: What happened?
   B: Some neighborhood kids were playing baseball, and their ball went through the glass.

★*I bought a few apples.* = I bought a small number of apples.
I bought a little apple. = I bought one apple, and it was small, not large.

Count/Noncount Nouns and Articles **299**

11-6 Nouns That Can Be Count or Noncount

Quite a few nouns can be used as either count or noncount nouns. Examples of both count and noncount usages for some common nouns follow.

Noun	Used as a Noncount Noun	Used as a Count Noun
glass	(a) Windows are made of *glass*.	(b) I drank *a glass* of water. (c) Janet wears *glasses* when she reads.
hair	(d) Rita has brown *hair*.	(e) There's *a hair* on my jacket.
iron	(f) *Iron* is a metal.	(g) I pressed my shirt with *an iron*.
light	(h) I opened the curtain to let in *some light*.	(i) Please turn off *the lights* (*lamps*).
paper	(j) I need *some paper* to write a note.	(k) I wrote *a paper* for Professor Lee. (l) I bought *a paper* (*a newspaper*).
time	(m) How *much time* do you need to finish your work?	(n) How *many times* have you been to Mexico?
work	(o) I have *some work* to do tonight.	(p) That painting is *a work* of art.
coffee	(q) I had *some coffee* after dinner.	(r) *Two coffees*, please.
chicken/fish	(s) I ate *some chicken/some fish*.	(t) She drew a picture of *a chicken/a fish*.
experience	(u) I haven't had *much experience* with computers. (I don't have much knowledge or skill in using computers.)	(v) I had *many* interesting *experiences* on my trip. (Many interesting events happened to me on my trip.)

❏ **Exercise 21. Looking at grammar.** (Chart 11-6)
Match the correct picture to each sentence on page 301. Discuss the differences in meaning.

Picture A   Picture B   Picture C

Picture D   Picture E   Picture F

1. That was a great meal. I ate a lot of chicken. Now I'm stuffed.* _____
2. Are you hungry? How about a little chicken for lunch? _____
3. When I was a child, we raised a lot of chickens. _____
4. I bought a few chickens so I can have fresh eggs. _____
5. There's a little chicken in your yard. _____
6. That's a big chicken over there. Who does it belong to? _____

☐ **Exercise 22. Looking at grammar.** (Chart 11-6)
Complete the sentences with the given words. Make words plural as necessary. Choose words in parentheses as necessary. Discuss the differences in meaning.

1. time   It took a lot of __*time*__ to write my composition.

2. time   I really like that movie. I saw it three __*times*__ .

3. paper   Students in Professor Young's literature class have to write a lot of

     _____ .

4. paper   Students who take careful lecture notes can use a lot of _____ .

5. paper   The *New York Times* is (*a, some*) famous _____ .

6. work   Van Gogh's painting *Irises* is one of my favorite _____ of art.

7. work   I have a lot of _____ to do tomorrow at my office.

8. hair   Erin has straight _____ , and Mariam has curly

     _____ .

9. hair   Brian has a white cat. When I stood up from Brian's sofa, my black slacks

     were covered with short white _____ .

10. glass   I wear _____ for reading.

11. glass   In some countries, people use _____ for their tea; in other

     countries, they use cups.

12. glass   Many famous paintings are covered with _____ to protect them.

13. iron   _____ (*is, are*) necessary to animal and plant life.

14. iron   _____ (*is, are*) used to make clothes look neat.

---

*stuffed = very full

15. experience   My grandfather had a lot of interesting _____ in his long career as a diplomat.

16. experience   You should apply for the job at the electronics company because you have a lot of _____ in that field.

17. chicken   Joe, would you like (*a, some*) more _____?

18. chicken   My grandmother raises _____ in her yard.

19. light   There (*is, are*) a lot of _____ on the ceilings of the school building.

20. light   A: If you want to take a picture outside now, you'll need a flash. The _____ (*isn't, aren't*) good here.

               B: Or, we could wait an hour. (*It, They*) will be brighter then.

❑ **Exercise 23. Warm-up.** (Chart 11-7)
Which of the following do you have in your kitchen? Check (✓) the items.

1. _____ a can* of tuna
2. _____ a bag of flour
3. _____ a jar of olive oil
4. _____ a bottle of soda pop
5. _____ a box of tea bags
6. _____ a bowl of sugar

11-7 Using Units of Measure with Noncount Nouns	
(a) I had some tea. (b) I had *two cups of tea*.	To mention a specific quantity of a noncount noun, speakers use units of measure such as *two cups of* or *one piece of*. A unit of measure usually describes **the container** (*a cup of, a bowl of*), **the amount** (*a pound of, a quart of*),* or **the shape** (*a bar of soap, a sheet of paper*).
(c) I ate some toast. (d) I ate *one piece of toast*.	

*Weight measure: *one pound* = 0.45 kilograms/kilos.
Liquid measure: *one quart* = 0.95 litres/liters; four quarts = one gallon = 3.8 litres/liters.

_____

*a can in American English = a tin in British English

Exercise 24. Looking at grammar. (Chart 11-7)

What units of measure are usually used with the given nouns? More than one unit of measure can be used with some of the nouns.

Part I. At the store

bag	bottle	box	can	jar

1. a ___can/jar___ of olives

2. a ___box___ of crackers

3. a _____ of mineral water

4. a _____ of jam or jelly

5. a _____ of tuna

6. a _____ of soup

7. a _____ of sugar

8. a _____ of wine

9. a _____ of soda

10. a _____ of flour

11. a _____ of paint

12. a _____ of breakfast cereal

Part II. In the kitchen

bowl	cup	glass	piece	slice

13. a ___cup/glass___ of green tea

14. a ___bowl___ of cereal

15. a _____ of candy

16. a _____ of bread

17. a _____ of cake

18. a _____ of orange juice

19. a _____ of soup

20. a _____ of pizza

| bowl | cup | glass | piece | slice |

21. a _____ of soda

22. a _____ of noodles

23. a _____ of mineral water

24. a _____ of popcorn

25. a _____ of cheese

26. a _____ of rice

27. a _____ of strawberries

28. a _____ of watermelon

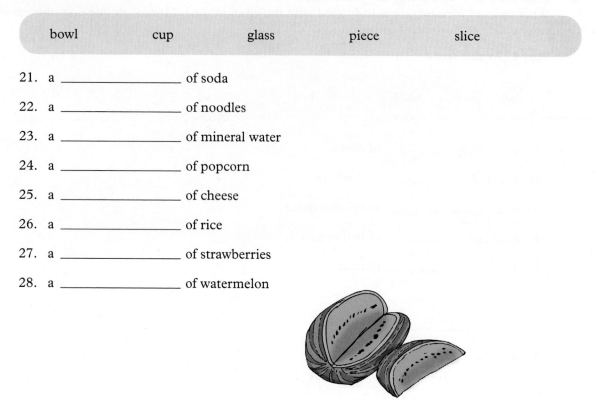

watermelon

❑ **Exercise 25. Let's talk.** (Chart 11-7)
You and your partner are planning a party for the class. You have already prepared most of the food, but you still need to buy a few things at the store. Decide what you'd like to get using the sentences below as your guide. You can be serious or silly. Perform your conversation for the class. Then your classmates will tell you if they want to come to your party or not.
NOTE: You can look at your conversation before you speak. When you speak, look at your partner.

Shopping list

A: So what else do we need from the store?

B: Let's see. We need a few jars of _____. We should also get a box of

_____. Oh, and a couple of bags of _____.

A: Is that it? Anything else?

B: I guess a few cans of _____ would be good.

I almost forgot. What should we do about drinks?

A: How about some bottles (or cans) of _____?

B: Good idea.

A: By the way, I thought we could serve slices of _____. How does that sound?

B: Sure.

Read the conversations. Why does Speaker A use *a* or *the?* Discuss what both Speaker A and Speaker B are thinking about.

Conversation 1

A: *A dog* makes a good pet. B: I agree.

Conversation 2

A: I saw *a dog* in my yard B: Oh?

Conversation 3

A: Did you feed *the dog?* B: Yes.

11-8 Guidelines for Article Usage

<table>
<tr><td colspan="2" align="center">TO MAKE A GENERALIZATION</td></tr>
<tr><td colspan="2">Singular Count Nouns: A/An</td></tr>
<tr>
<td>
(a) A dog makes a good pet.
(b) An apple is red.
(c) A pencil contains lead.
</td>
<td>In (a): The speaker is talking about any dog, all dogs, dogs in general.</td>
</tr>
<tr><td colspan="2">Plural Count Nouns: Ø</td></tr>
<tr>
<td>
(d) Ø Dogs make good pets.
(e) Ø Apples are red.
(f) Ø Pencils contain lead.
</td>
<td>In (d): The speaker is talking about any dog, all dogs, dogs in general.

NOTE: Examples (a) and (d) have the same meaning.</td>
</tr>
<tr><td colspan="2">Noncount Nouns: Ø</td></tr>
<tr>
<td>
(g) Ø Fruit is good for you.
(h) Ø Coffee contains caffeine.
(i) I like Ø music.
</td>
<td>In (g): The speaker is talking about any fruit, all fruit, fruit in general.</td>
</tr>
<tr><td colspan="2" align="center">TO TALK ABOUT NON-SPECIFIC PERSON(S) OR THING(S)</td></tr>
<tr><td colspan="2">Singular Count Nouns: A/An</td></tr>
<tr>
<td>
(j) I saw a dog in my yard.
(k) Mary ate an apple.
(l) I need a pencil.
</td>
<td>In (j): The speaker is saying, "I saw one dog (not two dogs, some dogs, many dogs). It wasn't a specific dog (e.g., your dog, the neighbor's dog, that dog). It was only one dog out of the whole group of animals called dogs."</td>
</tr>
<tr><td colspan="2">Plural Count Nouns: Some</td></tr>
<tr>
<td>
(m) I saw some dogs in my yard.
(n) Mary bought some apples.
(o) Bob has some pencils in his pocket.
</td>
<td>In (m): The speaker is saying, "I saw more than one dog. They weren't specific dogs (e.g., your dogs, the neighbor's dogs, those dogs). The exact number of dogs isn't important (two dogs, five dogs); I'm simply saying that I saw an indefinite number of dogs."

See Chart 11-5 for other words that can be used with plural count nouns, such as several, a few, and a lot of.</td>
</tr>
<tr><td colspan="2">Noncount Nouns: Some</td></tr>
<tr>
<td>
(p) I bought some fruit.
(q) Bob drank some coffee.
(r) Would you like to listen to some music?
</td>
<td>In (p): The speaker is saying, "I bought an indefinite amount of fruit. The exact amount (e.g., two pounds of fruit, four bananas, and two apples) isn't important. And I'm not talking about specific fruit (e.g., that fruit, the fruit in that bowl.)"

See Chart 11-5 for other words that can be used with noncount nouns, such as a little and a lot of.</td>
</tr>
</table>

11-8 Guidelines for Article Usage (continued)

THE SPEAKER AND THE LISTENER ARE THINKING ABOUT THE SAME SPECIFIC PERSON(S) OR THINGS.

Singular Count Nouns: *The*

(s) Did you feed *the* dog?
 (t) Kay is in *the kitchen.*
 (u) *The sun* is shining.
 (v) Please close *the door.*
 (w) *The president* is speaking on TV tonight.
 	
 (x) I had a banana and an apple. I gave *the banana* to Mary.
	In (s): The speaker and the listener are thinking about the same specific dog. The listener knows which dog the speaker is talking about: the dog that they own, the dog that they feed every day. There is only one dog that the speaker could possibly be talking about.
	
	 In (x): A speaker uses *the* when she/he mentions a noun the second time.
	   First mention: *I had **a banana** . . .*
	   Second mention: *I gave **the banana** . . .*
	
	 In the second mention, the listener now knows which banana the speaker is talking about: the banana the speaker had (not the banana John had, not the banana in that bowl).

Plural Count Nouns: *The*

(y) Did you feed *the dogs*? (z) *The pencils* on that desk are Jim's. (aa) Please turn off *the lights.* (bb) I had some bananas and apples. I gave *the bananas* to Mary.	In (y): The speaker and the listener are thinking about more than one dog, and they are thinking about the same specific dogs. In (bb) *the* is used for second mention.

Noncount Nouns: *The*

(cc) *The fruit* in this bowl is ripe. (dd) I can't hear you. *The music* is too loud. (ee) *The air* smells fresh today. (ff) I drank some coffee and some milk. *The coffee* was hot.	When *the* is used with noncount nouns, the speaker knows or can assume the listener is familiar with and thinking about the same specific thing. In (ff): *the* is used for second mention. NOTE: *a*, *an*, and *Ø* are not possible for the situations described in (s) through (ff).

□ **Exercise 27. Looking at grammar.** (Chart 11-8)
Read the following conversations and answer the questions that follow.

Conversation 1

A: **Dogs** make good pets.   B: I agree.

Conversation 2

A: I saw **some dogs** in my yard.   B: Oh?

Conversation 3

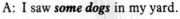

A: Did you feed **the dogs**?   B: Yes.

1. In which conversation are the speakers thinking about all dogs?
2. In which conversation are the speakers talking about the same dogs?
3. In which conversation are the speakers talking about an indefinite number of dogs?

Conversation 4

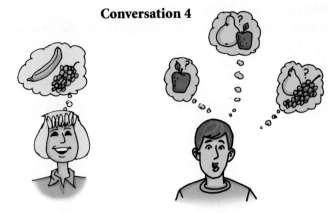

A: I ate *some fruit*.   B: Oh?

Conversation 5

A: *Fruit* is good for you.   B: I agree.

Conversation 6

A: *The fruit* in this bowl is ripe.   B: Good.

4. In which conversation are the speakers talking about all fruit?
5. In which conversation are the speakers talking about an indefinite amount of fruit?
6. In which conversation are the speakers thinking about the same fruit?

❑ **Exercise 28. Looking at grammar.** (Chart 11-8)
Read the conversations and decide whether the speakers would probably use **_the_** or **_a/an_**.

1. A: What did you do last night?

   B: I went to ___a___ party.

   A: Oh? Where was it?

2. A: Did you have a good time at ___the___ party last night?

   B: Yes.

   A: So did I. I'm glad that you decided to go with me.

3. A: Do you have _____ car?

   B: No. But I have _____ motorcycle.

4. A: Do you need _____ car today, honey?

   B: Yes. I have a lot of errands to do. Why don't I drive you to work today?

   A: Okay. But be sure to fill _____ car up with gas sometime today.

5. A: Have you seen my keys?

   B: Yes. They're on _____ table next to _____ front door.

6. A: Where's _____ professor?

   B: She's absent today.

7. A: Is Mr. Jones _____ graduate student?

   B: No. He's _____ professor.

8. A: Would you like to go to _____ zoo this afternoon?

   B: Sure. Why not?

9. A: Does San Diego have _____ zoo?

   B: Yes. It's world famous.

10. A: Where's Dennis?

    B: He's in _____ kitchen.

11. A: Do you like your new apartment?

    B: Yes. It has _____ big kitchen.

12. A: Did you lock _____ door?

    B: Yes.

    A: Did you check _____ stove?

    B: Yes.

    A: Did you close all _____ windows downstairs?

B: Yes.

A: Did you set _____ alarm clock?

B: Yes.

A: Then let's turn out _____ lights.

B: Goodnight, dear.

A: Oh, don't forget your appointment with _____ doctor tomorrow.

B: Yes, dear. Goodnight.

❑ Exercise 29. Looking at grammar. (Chart 11-8)

Decide if the **boldface** noun is singular, plural, or noncount. Then decide if it has a general or specific meaning.

	Singular	Plural	Noncount	General	Specific
1. **Birds** have feathers.		X		X	
2. A **bird** has feathers.					
3. A bird eats **worms**.					
4. A **worm** lives under the ground.					
5. Birds and worms need **water**.					
6. The **bird** is drinking water.					
7. The **birds** are drinking water.					
8. The **water** is on the ground.					

❑ Exercise 30. Looking at grammar. (Chart 11-8)

Complete the sentences with the given nouns. Use **the** for specific statements. Do not use **the** for general statements.

1. flowers a. ___The flowers___ in that vase are beautiful.

   b. ___Flowers___ are beautiful.

2. mountains a. _____ are beautiful.

   b. _____ in Switzerland are beautiful.

3. water a. I don't want to go swimming today. _____ is too cold.

   b. _____ consists of hydrogen and oxygen.

4. information a. _____ in this magazine article is upsetting.

   b. The Internet is a widely used source of _____.

5. health a. _____ is more important than money.

   b. Doctors are concerned with _____ of their patients.

6. men   a. _____ generally have stronger muscles than

     women   _____ .

            b. At the party last night, _____ sat on one side of the

               room, and _____ sat on the other.

7. problems   a. Everyone has _____ .

            b. Irene told me about _____ she had with her car

               yesterday.

8. vegetables   a. _____ we had for dinner last night

               were overcooked.

            b. _____ are good for you.

☐ **Exercise 31. Reading.** (Chart 11-8)
Read the passage. Then cover it with a piece of paper and complete the sentences.

Money

     In ancient times, people did not use coins for money. Instead, shells, beads, or salt were used. Around 2,600 years ago, the first metal coins were made. Today most money is made from paper. Of course, many people use plastic credit or debit cards to pay for goods. In the future, maybe we'll use only cards, and paper money won't exist.

1. In ancient times, two forms of money were _____ .

2. People first made _____ 2,600 years ago.

3. Nowadays, paper is used for _____ .

4. Today people can pay for goods with _____ or _____ .

5. In the future, _____ may replace _____ .

☐ **Exercise 32. Looking at grammar.** (Chart 11-8)
Complete the sentences with *the* or Ø. Capitalize the beginning of sentences as necessary.

1. __Ø__ B̶utter is a dairy product.

2. Please pass me _____ butter.

3. _____ air is humid today.

4. When I was in Memorial Hospital, _____ nurses were wonderful.

5. I'm studying _____ grammar. I'm also studying _____ vocabulary.

6. _____ trees reduce _____ pollution by cleaning the air.

7. _____ trees in my yard are 200 years old.

❑ **Exercise 33. Looking at grammar.** (Chart 11-8)
Complete the sentences with *a/an*, *the*, or *some*.

1. I had __*a*__ banana and __*an*__ apple. I gave __*the*__ banana to Mary. I ate __*the*__ apple.

2. I had _____ bananas and _____ apples. I gave _____ bananas to Mary. I ate _____ apples.

3. I forgot to bring my things with me to class yesterday, so I borrowed _____ pen and _____ paper from Joe. I returned _____ pen, but I used _____ paper for my homework.

4. A: What did you do last weekend?
   B: I went on _____ picnic Saturday and saw _____ movie Sunday.
   A: Did you have fun?
   B: _____ picnic was fun, but _____ movie was boring.

5. I bought _____ bag of flour and _____ sugar to make _____ cookies. _____ sugar was okay, but I had to return _____ flour. When I opened it, I found _____ little bugs in it. I took it back to the people at the store and showed them _____ little bugs. They gave me _____ new bag of flour. _____ new bag didn't have any bugs in it.

❑ **Exercise 34. Listening.** (Chart 11-8)
Listen to the passage. Then listen again and write *a/an*, *the*, or *Ø*. Before you begin, you may want to check your understanding of these words: *roof (of your mouth)*, *nerves*, *blood vessels*, *avoid*.

Ice-Cream Headaches

Have you ever eaten something really cold like ice cream and suddenly gotten __*a*__
                                                                                  1
headache? This is known as _____ "ice-cream headache." About 30 percent of the
                                    2
population gets this type of _____ headache. Here is one theory about why _____
                                  3   4

ice-cream headaches occur. _____ roof of your mouth has a lot of nerves. When
                                    5

something cold touches these nerves, they want to warm up _____ your brain. They
                                                                    6

make _____ your blood vessels swell up (get bigger), and this causes _____ lot of pain.
        7   8

_____ ice-cream headaches generally go away after about 30–60 seconds. _____ best
      9   10

way to avoid these headaches is to keep cold food off _____ roof of your mouth.
                                                               11

❑ **Exercise 35. Looking at grammar.** (Chapter 11-8)
   Write *a/an, the,* or **Ø** in the blanks.

1. I have ___*a*___ window in my bedroom. I keep it open at night because I like fresh air.

   ___*The*___ window is above my bed.

2. Kathy likes to listen to _____ music when she studies.

3. Would you please turn _____ radio down? _____ music is too loud.

4. Last week I read _____ book about _____ life of Indira Gandhi, India's only
   female prime minister, who was assassinated in 1984.

5. Let's go swimming in _____ lake today.

6. _____ water is essential to human life, but don't drink _____ water in the Flat
   River. It'll kill you! _____ pollution in that river is terrible.

7. People can drink _____ fresh water. They can't drink _____ seawater because it
   contains _____ salt.

8. Ted, pass _____ salt, please. And _____ pepper. Thanks.

9. A: How did you get here? Did you walk?
   B: No, I took _____ taxi.

10. A: Wow! What a great meal!
    B: I agree. _____ food was excellent — especially _____ fish. And _____
       service was exceptionally good. Let's leave _____ waitress a good tip.

11. A: Kids, get in _____ car, please.
    B: We can't. _____ doors are locked.

Exercise 36. Warm-up. (Chart 11-9)
Complete the questions with *the* or Ø.

Would you like to see . . .

1. ___the___ Amazon River?

2. ___Ø___ Korea?

3. _____ Mexico City?

4. _____ Indian Ocean?

5. _____ Ural Mountains?

6. _____ Australia?

7. _____ Mississippi River?

8. _____ Red Sea?

9. _____ Lake Michigan?

10. _____ Mount Fuji?

11-9 Using *The* or Ø with Names

(a) We met Ø *Mr. Wang*. I know Ø *Doctor Smith*. Ø *President Rice* has been in the news.	***The*** is NOT used with titled names. *INCORRECT:* We met the Mr. Wang.
(b) He lives in Ø *Europe*. Ø *Asia* is the largest continent. Have you ever been to Ø *Africa*?	***The*** is NOT used with the names of continents. *INCORRECT:* He lives in the Europe.
(c) He lives in Ø *France*. Ø *Brazil* is a large country. Have you ever been to Ø *Thailand*?	***The*** is NOT used with the names of most countries. *INCORRECT:* He lives in the France. ***The*** is used in the names of only a few countries, as in (d). Others: *the Czech Republic, the United Arab Emirates, the Dominican Republic.*
(d) He lives in ***the*** *United States*. ***The*** *Netherlands* is in Europe. Have you ever been to ***the*** *Philippines*?	
(e) He lives in Ø *Paris*. Ø *New York* is the largest city in the United States. Have you ever been to Ø *Istanbul*?	***The*** is NOT used with the names of cities. *INCORRECT:* He lives in the Paris.
(f) ***The*** *Nile River* is long. They crossed ***the*** *Pacific Ocean*. ***The*** *Yellow Sea* is in Asia.	***The*** is used with the names of rivers, oceans, and seas. ***The*** is NOT used with the names of lakes.
(g) Chicago is on Ø *Lake Michigan*. Ø *Lake Titicaca* lies on the border between Peru and Bolivia.	
(h) We hiked in ***the*** *Alps*. ***The*** *Andes* are in South America.	***The*** is used with the names of mountain ranges. ***The*** is NOT used with the names of individual mountains.
(i) He climbed Ø *Mount Everest*. Ø *Mount Fuji* is in Japan.	

❑ **Exercise 37. Game: trivia.** (Chart 11-9)
Work in teams. Complete the sentences with **the** or **Ø**. Then decide if the statements are true or false. Circle "T" for true and "F" for false. The team with the most correct answers wins.*

1. _____ Moscow is the biggest city _____ Russia.   T   F

2. _____ Rhine River flows through _____ Germany.   T   F

3. _____ Vienna is in _____ Australia.   T   F

4. _____ Yangtze is the longest river in _____ Asia.   T   F

5. _____ Atlantic Ocean is bigger than _____ Pacific.   T   F

6. _____ Rocky Mountains are located in _____ Canada
   and _____ United States.   T   F

7. _____ Dr. Sigmund Freud is famous for his studies of astronomy.   T   F

8. _____ Lake Victoria is located in _____ Tanzania.   T   F

9. Another name for _____ Holland is _____ Netherlands.   T   F

10. _____ Swiss Alps are the tallest mountains in the world.   T   F

❑ **Exercise 38. Game.** (Chart 11-9)
Work in groups. Choose a place in the world. It can be a continent, country, city, sea, river, mountain, etc. Your classmates will try to guess where it is by asking *yes/no* questions. Limit the number of questions to ten for each place.

Example:
SPEAKER A: (*thinking of the Mediterranean Sea*)
SPEAKER B: Is it a continent?
SPEAKER A: No.
SPEAKER C: Is it hot?
SPEAKER A: No.
SPEAKER D: Is it big?
SPEAKER A: Yes.
Etc.

❑ **Exercise 39. Warm-up.** (Chart 11-10)
Complete the sentences with information about yourself.

1. I was born in _____ .
                         (continent)

2. I have lived most of my life in _____ .
                                         (country)

3. This term I am studying _____ .

4. Two of my favorite movies are _____ and

   _____ .

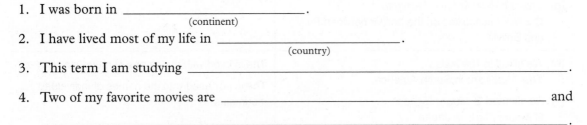

---

*See *Trivia Answers*, p. 421.

11-10 Capitalization

Capitalize

1. The first word of a sentence	We saw a movie last night. It was very good.	*Capitalize* = use a big letter, not a small letter
2. The names of people	I met George Adams yesterday.	
3. Titles used with the names of people	I saw Doctor (Dr.) Smith. There's Professor (Prof.) Lee.	I saw a doctor. BUT I saw Doctor Wilson.
4. Months, days, holidays	I was born in April. Bob arrived last Monday. It snowed on New Year's Day.	NOTE: Seasons are not capitalized: *spring, summer, fall/autumn, winter.*

5. The names of places:
    city
    state/province
    country
    continent
	He lives in Chicago.
	She was born in California.
	They are from Mexico.
	Tibet is in Asia.
		She lives in a city. BUT
		She lives in New York City.

ocean
    lake
    river
    desert
    mountain
	They crossed the Atlantic Ocean.
	Chicago is on Lake Michigan.
	The Nile River flows north.
	The Sahara Desert is in Africa.
	We visited the Rocky Mountains.
		They crossed a river.
		They crossed the Yellow River.

school business	I go to the University of Florida. I work for the Boeing Company.	I go to a university. BUT I go to the University of Texas.

street
    building
    park, zoo
	He lives on Grand Avenue.
	We have class in Ritter Hall.
	I went jogging in Forest Park.
		We went to a park. BUT
		We went to Central Park.

6. The names of courses	I'm taking Chemistry 101.	Here's your history book. BUT I'm taking History 101.
7. The titles of books, articles, movies	*Gone with the Wind* *The Sound of the Mountain*	Capitalize the first word of a title. Capitalize all other words except articles (*the, a/an*), coordinating conjunctions (*and, but, or*), and short prepositions (*with, in, at, etc.*).
8. The names of languages and nationalities	She speaks Spanish. We discussed Japanese customs.	Words that refer to the names of languages and nationalities are always capitalized.
9. The names of religions	Buddhism, Christianity, Hinduism, Islam, and Judaism are major religions in the world. Talal is a Muslim.	Words that refer to the names of religions are always capitalized.

Exercise 40. Looking at grammar. (Chart 11-10)
Add capital letters where necessary. Some sentences need no changes.

                             T

1. We're going to have a test next tuesday.

2. Do you know richard smith? he is a professor at this university.

3. I know that professor smith teaches at the university of arizona.

4. Where was your mother born?

5. John is a catholic. ali is a muslem.

6. Anita speaks french. she studied in france for two years.

7. I'm taking a history course this semester.

8. I'm taking modern european history 101 this semester.

9. We went to vancouver, british columbia, for our vacation last summer.

10. Venezuela is a spanish-speaking country.

11. Canada is in north america.★

12. Canada is north of the united states.

13. The sun rises in the east.

14. The mississippi river flows south.

15. The amazon is a river in south america.

16. We went to a zoo. We went to brookfield zoo in chicago.

17. The title of this book is *fundamentals of english grammar.*

18. I enjoy studying english grammar.

19. On valentine's day (february 14th), sweethearts give each other presents.

20. I read a book called *the cat and the mouse in my aunt's house.*

★When **north**, **south**, **east**, and **west** refer to the direction on a compass, they are not capitalized: *Japan is **east** of China.*
When they are part of a geographical name, they are capitalized: *Japan is in the Far **East**.*

❏ **Exercise 41. Grammar, reading, and writing.** (Chapter

Part I. Read the passage. Add capital letters as necessary.

Jane Goodall

(1) Do you recognize the name ɉane goodall? Perhaps you know her for her studies of chimpanzees. She became very famous from her work in tanzania.

(2) Jane goodall was born in england, and as a child, was fascinated by animals. Her favorite books were *the jungle book,* by rudyard kipling, and books about tarzan, a fictional character who was raised by apes.

(3) Her childhood dream was to go to africa. After high school, she worked as a secretary and a waitress to earn enough money to go there. During that time, she took evening courses in journalism and english literature. She saved every penny until she had enough money for a trip to africa.

(4) In the spring of 1957, she sailed through the red sea and southward down the african coast to mombasa in kenya. Her uncle had arranged a job for her in nairobi with a british company. When she was there, she met dr. louis leakey, a famous anthropologist. Under his guidance, she began her lifelong study of chimpanzees on the eastern shore of lake tanganyika.

(5) Jane goodall lived alone in a tent near the lake. Through months and years of patience, she won the trust of the chimps and was able to watch them closely. Her observations changed forever how we view chimpanzees — and all other animals we share the world with.

the passage again and then read these statements. Circle "T" for true and "F"

...ne Goodall was interested in animals from an early age.	T	F
Her parents paid for her trip to Africa.	T	F
3. She studied animals in zoos as well as chimpanzees in the wild.	T	F
4. Dr. Leakey was helpful to Jane Goodall.	T	F
5. Jane studied chimpanzees with many other people.	T	F
6. Goodall's work changed how chimpanzees look at the world.	T	F

Part III. Read the sample paragraph about the organization called Roots and Shoots. Then write your own paragraph about an organization that is doing something to help people or animals. Focus on correct article usage and capitalization. Note the articles in green in the passage. Follow these steps:

(1) Choose an organization you are interested in.

(2) Research the organization. Find the organization's website if possible. Take notes on the information you find. Include information about its history, why it was formed, the person or people who formed it, and its goals.

(3) Review Chart 11-10 and check your paragraph for proper capitalization.

(4) Edit your paragraph for article use. You may also want to ask another student to read it.

Example:

Roots and Shoots

Jane Goodall went to Africa to study animals. She spent 40 years observing and studying chimpanzees in Tanzania. As a result of Dr. Goodall's work, an organization called Roots and Shoots was formed. This organization focuses on work children and teenagers can do to help the local and global community. The idea began in 1991. A group of 16 teenagers met with Dr. Goodall at her home in Dar Es Salaam, Tanzania. They wanted to discuss how to help with a variety of problems, such as pollution, deforestation, the treatment of animals, and the future of wildlife, like Dr. Goodall's chimpanzees. Dr. Goodall was involved in the meetings, but the teenagers chose the service projects and did the work themselves. The first Roots and Shoots community project was a local one. The group educated villagers about better treatment of chickens at home and in the marketplace. Today, there are tens of thousands of members in almost 100 countries. They work to make their environment and the world a better place through community-service projects.

Chapter 12
Adjective Clauses

□ **Exercise 1. Warm-up.** (Chart 12-1)
Check (✓) the completions that are true for you.

I have a friend who . . .

1. ____ lives near me.
2. ____ is interested in soccer.
3. ____ likes to do exciting things.
4. ____ is studying to be an astronaut.

12-1 Adjective Clauses: Introduction

Adjectives	Adjective Clauses
An **adjective** modifies a noun. *Modify* means to change a little. An adjective describes or gives information about the noun. (See Chart 6-8, p. 160.)	An **adjective clause*** modifies a noun. It describes or gives information about a noun.
An adjective usually comes in front of a noun.	An adjective clause follows a noun.

(a) I met a <u>adjective</u> + <u>noun</u>
   kind   man'.
	(c) I met a <u>noun</u> + <u>adjective clause</u>
	   man' *who is kind to everybody*.

(b) I met a <u>adjective</u> + <u>noun</u>
   famous   man'.
	(d) I met a <u>noun</u> + <u>adjective clause</u>
	   man' *who is a famous poet*.

	(e) I met a <u>noun</u> + <u>adjective clause</u> man' *who lives in Chicago*.

---

*GRAMMAR TERMINOLOGY

(1) **I met a man** = an independent clause; it is a complete sentence. (2) **He lives in Chicago** = an independent clause; it is a complete sentence. (3) **who lives in Chicago** = a dependent clause; it is NOT a complete sentence. (4) **I met a man who lives in Chicago** = an independent clause + a dependent clause; a complete sentence.	A **clause** is a structure that has a subject and a verb. There are two kinds of clauses: **independent** and **dependent**. • An **independent clause** is a main clause and can stand alone as a sentence, as in (1) and (2). • A **dependent clause**, as in (3), cannot stand alone as a sentence. It must be connected to an independent clause, as in (4).

❑ **Exercise 2. Looking at grammar.** (Chart 12-1)
Check (✓) the items that have complete sentences.

1. _____ I know a teenager. She flies airplanes.
2. _____ I know a teenager who flies airplanes.
3. _____ A teenager who flies airplanes.
4. _____ Who flies airplanes.
5. _____ Who flies airplanes?
6. _____ I know a teenager flies airplanes.

❑ **Exercise 3. Warm-up.** (Chart 12-2)
Complete the sentences with the correct words from the list. <u>Underline</u> the word that follows *doctor* in each sentence.

| A dermatologist | An orthopedist | A pediatrician | A surgeon |

1. _____ is a doctor who performs operations.
2. _____ is a doctor that treats skin problems.
3. _____ is a doctor who treats bone injuries.
4. _____ is a doctor that treats children.

12-2 Using *Who* and *That* in Adjective Clauses to Describe People

(a) The man is friendly.	S V *He* lives next to me. ↓ *who* ↓ S V *who* lives next to me	In adjective clauses, **who** and **that** are used as subject pronouns to describe people. In (a): **He** is a subject pronoun. **He** refers to "the man." To make an adjective clause, change **he** to **who**. **Who** is a subject pronoun. **Who** refers to "the man."
(b) The man **who** *lives next to me* is friendly.		
(c) The woman is talkative.	S V *She* lives next to me. ↓ *that* ↓ S V *that* lives next to me	**That** is also a subject pronoun and can replace **who**, as in (d). The subject pronouns **who** and **that** cannot be omitted from an adjective clause. *INCORRECT: The woman lives next to me is talkative.* As subject pronouns, both **who** and **that** are common in conversation, but **who** is more common in writing.
(d) The woman **that** *lives next to me* is talkative.	In (b) and (d): The adjective clause immediately follows the noun it modifies. *INCORRECT: The woman is talkative that lives next to me.*	

□ **Exercise 4. Looking at grammar.** (Chart 12-2)
Circle the <u>two</u> sentences that express the ideas in the given sentence.

1. The librarian who helped me with my research lives near my parents.
   a. The librarian lives near my parents.
   b. I live near my parents.
   c. The librarian helped my parents.
   d. The librarian helped me.

2. The veterinarian that took care of my daughter's goat was very gentle.
   a. The veterinarian took care of my goat.
   b. The goat was gentle.
   c. The veterinarian treated my daughter's goat.
   d. The veterinarian was gentle.

□ **Exercise 5. Looking at grammar.** (Charts 12-1 and 12-2)
<u>Underline</u> each adjective clause. Draw an arrow to the noun it modifies.

1. The hotel clerk <u>who gave us our room keys</u> speaks several languages.

2. The manager that hired me has less experience than I do.

3. I like the manager that works in the office next to mine.

4. My mother is a person who wakes up every morning with a positive attitude.

5. A person who wakes up with a positive attitude every day is lucky.

□ **Exercise 6. Looking at grammar.** (Charts 12-1 and 12-2)
Change the b. sentences to adjective clauses. Combine each pair of sentences with **who** or **that**.

Example: a. Do you know the people?   b. They live in the house on the corner.
   → *Do you know the people **who** (or **that**) live in the white house?*

1. a. The police officer was friendly.   b. She gave me directions.

2. a. The waiter was slow.   b. He served us dinner.

3. a. I talked to the women.   b. They walked into my office.

4. a. The man talked a lot.   b. He sat next to me on the plane.

5. a. The people have three cars.   b. They live next to me.

□ **Exercise 7. Looking at grammar.** (Charts 12-1 and 12-2)
Add **who** or **that** as necessary.

                                who
1. I liked the people ∧ sat next to us at the soccer game.

2. The man answered the phone was polite.

3. People paint houses for a living are called house painters.

4. I'm uncomfortable around married couples argue all the time.

5. While I was waiting at the bus stop, I stood next to an elderly man started a conversation with me about my school.

□ **Exercise 8. Let's talk.** (Charts 12-1 and 12-2)
Work in pairs or small groups. Complete the sentences. Make true statements. Share some of your sentences with the class.

1. I know a man/woman who . . . .
2. I have a friend who . . . .
3. I like athletes who . . . .
4. Workers who . . . are brave.
5. People who . . . make me laugh.
6. Doctors who . . . are admirable.

□ **Exercise 9. Warm-up.** (Chart 12-3)
Complete the sentences with your own words.

1. The teacher that I had for first grade was _____.

2. The first English teacher I had was _____.

3. The first English teacher who I had wasn't _____.

12-3 Using Object Pronouns in Adjective Clauses to Describe People

(a) The man was friendly. S V O I met *him*. ↓ *that*	In adjective clauses, pronouns are used as the object of a verb to describe people. In (a): *him* is an object pronoun. *Him* refers to "the man." One way to make an adjective clause is to change *him* to *that*. *That* is the object pronoun. *That* refers to "the man." *That* comes at the beginning of an adjective clause.
O S V (b) The man *that* *I met* was friendly. (c) The man Ø *I met* was friendly.	An object pronoun can be omitted from an adjective clause, as in (c).
S V O (d) The man was friendly. I met *him*. ↓ *who* *whom*	*Him* can also be changed to *who* or *whom*, as in (e) and (f). As an object pronoun, *that* is more common than *who* in speaking. Ø is the most common choice for both speaking and writing. *Whom* is generally used only in very formal writing.
O S V (e) The man *who* *I met* was friendly. (f) The man *whom* *I met* was friendly.	

❏ **Exercise 10. Looking at grammar.** (Charts 12-2 and 12-3)
Check (✓) the sentences that have object pronouns.

1. __✓__ The children who we invited to the party are from the neighborhood.
2. _____ The children that we invited to the party were excited to come.
3. _____ The children whom we invited to the party had a good time.
4. _____ The children who live next door are a lot of fun.
5. _____ Marie and Luis Escobar still keep in touch with many of the students that they met in their English class five years ago.
6. _____ People who listen to loud music on earphones can suffer gradual hearing loss.
7. _____ I know a couple who sailed around the world.
8. _____ The couple whom we had over for dinner sailed around the world.

❏ **Exercise 11. Looking at grammar.** (Charts 12-2 and 12-3)
Circle all the correct completions.

1. The woman _____ was interesting.
   a. that I met last night
   b. I met last night
   c. who I met last night
   d. whom I met last night

2. The man _____ was fast.
   a. that painted our house
   b. painted our house
   c. who painted our house
   d. whom painted

3. The people _____ live on Elm Street.
   a. that Nadia is visiting
   b. Nadia is visiting
   c. who Nadia is visiting
   d. whom Nadia is visiting

4. The students _____ missed the quiz.
   a. that came to class late
   b. came to class late
   c. who came to class late
   d. whom came to class late

❏ **Exercise 12. Looking at grammar.** (Chart 12-3)
Combine each pair of sentences with **that, who,** or **whom**. <u>Underline</u> the object pronouns in the b. sentences and change the sentences to adjective clauses.

Example: a. A woman asked me for my phone number   b. I didn't know <u>her</u>.
   → *A woman that/whom I didn't know asked me for my phone number.*

1. a. The couple was two hours late.   b. I invited them for dinner.

2. a. The man snored the entire flight.   b. I sat next to him on the plane.

3. a. The man tried to shoplift some groceries.   b. The police arrested him.

4. a. The chef is very experienced.   b. The company hired her.

□ **Exercise 13. Let's talk: pairwork.** (Charts 12-2 and 12-3)
Work with a partner. Take turns making adjective clauses by combining the given sentences with the main sentence.

Main sentence: The man was helpful.

1. He gave me directions. → *The man who/that gave me directions was helpful.*
2. He answered my question.
3. I called him.
4. You recommended him.
5. He is the owner.
6. You invited him to the party.
7. He was walking with his kids.
8. I saw him in the waiting room.
9. He sold us our museum tickets.
10. He gave us a discount.

□ **Exercise 14. Looking at grammar.** (Charts 12-2 and 12-3)
Complete the sentences with *that, Ø, who,* or *whom.* Write all the possible completions.

1. The man _____ married my mother is now my stepfather.

2. The man _____ my mother married is now my stepfather.

3. Do you know the boy _____ is talking to Anita?

4. I've become good friends with several of the people _____ I met in my English class last year.

5. A woman _____ I saw in the park was holding several balloons.

6. The woman _____ was holding several balloons was entertaining some children.

□ **Exercise 15. Warm-up.** (Chart 12-4)
Read the paragraph about James and then check (✓) the sentences that you agree with. What do you notice about the adjective clauses in green?

   James is looking for a pet. He is single and a little lonely. He isn't sure what kind of pet would be best for him. He lives on a large piece of property in the country. He is gone during the day from 8:00 A.M. to 5:00 P.M. but is home on weekends. He travels about two months a year but has neighbors that can take care of a pet, as long as it isn't too big. What kind of pet should he get?

1. _____ He should get a pet that likes to run and be outside, like a dog.
2. _____ He needs to get a pet which is easy to take care of, like a fish or turtle.
3. _____ He should get an animal that he can leave alone for a few days, like a horse.
4. _____ He needs to get an animal his neighbors will like.

12-4 Using Pronouns in Adjective Clauses to Describe Things

(a) The river is polluted. ⎡ S **It** ↓ **that** **which** ⎤ V flows through the town.	**Who** and **whom** refer to people. **Which** refers to things. **That** can refer to either people or things.
(b) The river **that** _flows through the town_ is polluted. **(c)** The river **which** _flows through the town_ is polluted.	In (a): To make an adjective clause, change **it** to **that** or **which**. **It, that,** and **which** all refer to a thing (the river). (b) and (c) have the same meaning, but (b) is more common than (c) in speaking and writing.
	When **that** and **which** are used as the subject of an adjective clause, they CANNOT be omitted. _INCORRECT:_ The river flows through the town is polluted.
(d) The books were expensive. I bought ⎡ O **them.** ↓ **that** **which** ⎤	**That** or **which** can be used as an object in an adjective clause, as in (e) and (f). An object pronoun can be omitted from an adjective clause, as in (g). (e), (f), and (g) have the same meaning. In speaking, **that** and Ø are more common than **which**. In writing, **that** is the most common, and Ø is rare.
(e) The books **that** _I bought_ were expensive. **(f)** The books **which** _I bought_ were expensive. **(g)** The books Ø _I bought_ were expensive.	

☐ **Exercise 16. Looking at grammar.** (Chart 12-4)
Underline each adjective clause. Draw an arrow to the noun it modifies.

1. I lost the scarf that I borrowed from my roommate.

2. The food we ate at the sidewalk café was delicious.

3. The bus that I take to school every morning is usually very crowded.

4. Pizza which is sold by the slice is a popular lunch in many cities throughout the world.

5. Piranhas are dangerous fish that can tear the flesh off an animal as large as a horse in a few minutes.

□ **Exercise 17. Looking at grammar.** (Chart 12-4)
Combine each pair of sentences into one sentence. Give all possible forms.

1. a. The pill made me sleepy.   b. I took it.
   → *The pill that I took made me sleepy.*
   → *The pill Ø I took made me sleepy.*
   → *The pill which I took made me sleepy.*

2. a. The soup was too salty.   b. I had it for lunch.

3. a. I have a class.   b. It begins at 8:00 A.M.

4. a. The information helped me a lot.   b. I found it on the Internet.

5. a. My daughter asked me a question.   b. I couldn't answer it.

6. a. Where can I catch the bus?   b. It goes downtown.

□ **Exercise 18. Looking at grammar.** (Charts 12-3 and 12-4)
Cross out the incorrect pronouns in the adjective clauses.

1. The books I bought ~~them~~ at the bookstore were expensive.

2. I like the shirt you wore it to class yesterday.

3. Amanda Jones is a person I would like you to meet her.

4. The apartment we wanted to rent it had two bedrooms.

5. My wife and I are really enjoying the TV set that we bought it for our anniversary.

6. The woman you met her at Aunt Barbara's house is an Olympic athlete.

7. Ayako has a cat that it likes to catch mice.

8. The mice that Ayako's cat catches them live in the basement.

□ **Exercise 19. Looking at grammar.** (Charts 12-2 → 12-4)
Write all the pronouns that can be used to connect the adjective clauses to the main clauses:
that, who, which, or ***whom.*** If the pronoun can be omitted, use **Ø**.

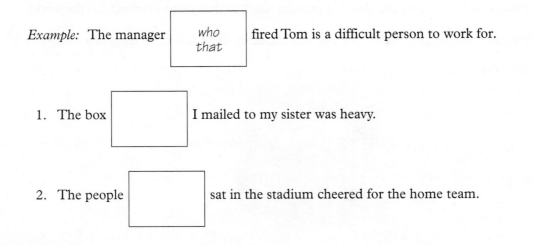

Example: The manager | *who*
that | fired Tom is a difficult person to work for.

1. The box | | I mailed to my sister was heavy.

2. The people | | sat in the stadium cheered for the home team.

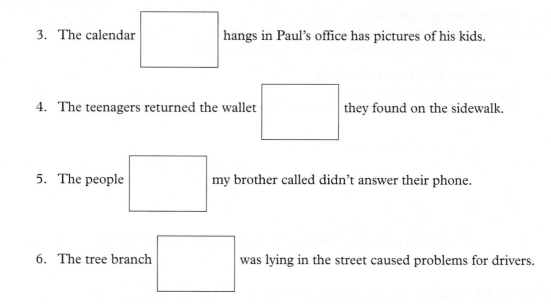

3. The calendar ☐ hangs in Paul's office has pictures of his kids.

4. The teenagers returned the wallet ☐ they found on the sidewalk.

5. The people ☐ my brother called didn't answer their phone.

6. The tree branch ☐ was lying in the street caused problems for drivers.

☐ **Exercise 20. Listening.** (Charts 12-2 → 12-4)
Listen to the sentences. They all have adjective clauses. Circle the words you hear. If there is no subject or object pronoun, choose **Ø**. NOTE: In spoken English, *that* often sounds like "thut."

My mother's hospital stay

Example: You will hear: The doctor who treated my mother was very knowledgeable.
You will choose: (who)   that   which   whom   Ø

1.	who	that	which	whom	Ø
2.	who	that	which	whom	Ø
3.	who	that	which	whom	Ø
4.	who	that	which	whom	Ø
5.	who	that	which	whom	Ø
6.	who	that	which	whom	Ø
7.	who	that	which	whom	Ø
8.	who	that	which	whom	Ø

☐ **Exercise 21. Let's talk.** (Charts 12-1 → 12-4)
Answer the questions in complete sentences. Use any appropriate pattern of adjective clause. Use **the** with the noun that is modified by the adjective clause.

1. • One phone wasn't ringing.
   • The other phone was ringing.
      QUESTIONS: Which phone did Hasan answer? Which phone didn't he answer?
      → *Hasan answered **the** phone that was ringing.*
      → *He didn't answer **the** phone that wasn't ringing.*

2. • One student raised her hand in class.
   • Another student sat quietly in his seat.
      QUESTIONS: Which student asked the teacher a question? Which one didn't?

3. • One girl won the bike race.
   • The other girl lost the bike race.
   QUESTIONS: Which girl is happy? Which girl isn't happy?

4. • We ate some food from our garden.
   • We ate some food at a restaurant.
   QUESTIONS: Which food was expensive? Which food wasn't expensive?

5. • One man was sleeping.
   • Another man was listening to the radio.
   QUESTIONS: Which man heard the special report about the earthquake in China? Which one didn't?

6. • One person bought a small car.
   • Another person bought a large car.
   QUESTIONS: Which person probably spent more money than the other?

❑ **Exercise 22. Game.** (Charts 12-3 and 12-4)
Work in teams. Complete each phrase in Column A with the correct phrase in Column B by using ***that*** or ***who***. Check your dictionary if necessary. The team that finishes first and has the most grammatically correct sentences wins.

Column A

1. A hammer is a tool . . . . *that is used to pound nails.*
2. A comedian is someone . . . .
3. An obstetrician is a doctor . . . .
4. Plastic is a chemical material . . . .
5. An architect is someone . . . .
6. A puzzle is a problem . . . .
7. A carnivore is an animal . . . .
8. Steam is a gas . . . .
9. A turtle is an animal . . . .
10. A hermit is a person . . . .
11. A pyramid is a structure . . . .

Column B

a. She/He leaves society and lives completely alone.
b. He/She tells jokes.
c. It forms when water boils.
d. It is square at the bottom and has four sides that come together in a point at the top.
e. She/He designs buildings.
f. He/She delivers babies.
✓g. It is used to pound nails.
h. It can be shaped and hardened to form many useful things.
i. It can be difficult to solve.
j. It eats meat.
k. It has a hard shell and can live in water or on land.

❑ **Exercise 23. Warm-up.** (Chart 12-5)
Read the sentences. What do you notice about the verbs in green and the nouns that precede them?

1. I have a friend who is vegetarian. He doesn't eat any meat.
2. I have friends who are vegetarian. They don't eat any meat.

12-5 Singular and Plural Verbs in Adjective Clauses

(a) I know the **man** who **is** sitting over there.	In (a): The verb in the adjective clause (**is**) is singular because **who** refers to a singular noun, **man**.
(b) I know the **people** who **are** sitting over there.	In (b): The verb in the adjective clause (**are**) is plural because **who** refers to a plural noun, **people**.

❑ **Exercise 24. Looking at grammar.** (Chart 12-5)
Circle the correct word in parentheses. <u>Underline</u> the noun that determines whether the verb should be singular or plural.

1. A saw is a <u>tool</u> that (*(is,)* *are*) used to cut wood.

2. Shovels are tools that (*is, are*) used to dig holes.

3. I recently met a woman that (*live, lives*) in Montreal.

4. Most people that (*live, lives*) in Montreal speak French as their first language.

5. I have a cousin who (*works, work*) as a coal miner.

6. Some coal miners that (*works, work*) underground suffer from lung disease.

7. A professional athlete who (*play, plays*) tennis is called a tennis pro.

8. Professional athletes who (*play, plays*) tennis for a living can make a lot of money.

9. Biographies are books which (*tells, tell*) the stories of people's lives.

10. A book that (*tells, tell*) the story of a person's life is called a biography.

11. I talked to the men who (*was, were*) sitting near me.

12. The woman that (*was, were*) sitting next to me at the movie was texting on her cell phone.

❑ **Exercise 25. Warm-up.** (Chart 12-6)
Complete the sentences with your own words.

1. A person that I recently spoke to was _____.

2. A person whom I recently spoke to wasn't _____.

3. The room which we are sitting in is _____.

4. The room we are sitting in has _____.

5. The room in which we are sitting doesn't have _____.

12-6 Using Prepositions in Adjective Clauses

(a) The man was nice. I talked **to** **him**. PREP OBJ	*That, whom,* and *which* can be used as the object (OBJ) of a preposition (PREP) in an adjective clause.

		OBJ		PREP	
(b)	The man	*that*	I talked	*to*	was nice.
(c)	The man	Ø	I talked	*to*	was nice.
(d)	The man	*whom*	I talked	*to*	was nice.

		PREP OBJ	
(e)	The man	*to whom* I talked	was nice.

REMINDER: An object pronoun can be omitted from an adjective clause, as in (c) and (h).

In very formal English, a preposition comes at the beginning of an adjective clause, followed by either *whom* or *which*, as in (e) and (j). This is not common in spoken English.

NOTE: In (e) and (j), *that* or *who* cannot be used, and the pronoun CANNOT be omitted.

(b), (c), (d), and (e) have the same meaning.

(g), (h), (i), and (j) have the same meaning.

				PREP	OBJ	
(f)	The chair is hard. I am sitting			*in*	*it*.	

		OBJ		PREP	
(g)	The chair	*that*	I am sitting	*in*	is hard.
(h)	The chair	Ø	I am sitting	*in*	is hard.
(i)	The chair	*which*	I am sitting	*in*	is hard.

		PREP	OBJ	
(j)	The chair	*in*	*which* I am sitting	is hard.

❑ **Exercise 26. Looking at grammar.** (Chart 12-6)
Change the b. sentences to adjective clauses. Combine each pair of sentences. Give all the possible forms of these clauses and <u>underline</u> them.

1. a. The movie was funny.   b. We went **to** it.
   → *The movie <u>that we went **to**</u> was funny.*
   → *The movie <u>Ø we went **to**</u> was funny.*
   → *The movie <u>which we went **to**</u> was funny.*
   → *The movie <u>**to** which we went</u> was funny.*

2. a. The man is over there.   b. I told you **about** him.

3. a. The woman pays me a fair salary. b. I work **for** her.

4. a. Alicia likes the family. b. She is living **with** them.

5. a. The picture is beautiful. b. Tom is looking **at** it.

6. a. I enjoyed the music. b. We listened **to** it after dinner.

❑ **Exercise 27. Looking at grammar.** (Chart 12-6)
Complete the sentences with appropriate prepositions.* Draw brackets around the adjective clauses.

1. I spoke __to__ a person. The person [I spoke __to__] was friendly.

2. We went _____ a movie. The movie we went _____ was very good.

3. We stayed _____ a motel. The motel we stayed _____ was clean and comfortable.

4. We listened _____ a new CD. I enjoyed the new CD we listened _____.

5. Sally was waiting _____ a person. The person Sally was waiting _____ never came.

6. I talked _____ a man. The man _____ whom I talked was helpful.

7. I never found the book that I was looking _____.

8. The interviewer wanted to know the name of the college I had graduated _____.

9. Oscar likes the Canadian family _____ whom he is staying.

10. The man who is staring _____ us looks unfriendly.

11. My sister and I have the same ideas about almost everything. She is the one person _____ whom I almost always agree.

12. What's the name of the person you introduced me _____ at the restaurant last night? I've already forgotten.

13. My father is someone I've always been able to depend _____ when I need advice or help.

14. The person you waved _____ is waving back at you.

15. Your building supervisor is the person _____ whom you should complain if you have any problems with your apartment.

*See Appendix Chart C-2 for a list of preposition combinations.

□ **Exercise 28. Listening.** (Charts 12-1 → 12-6)

Listen to the sentences and choose all the true statements.

Example: You will hear: The university I want to attend is in New York.
You will choose: (a.) I want to go to a university.
   b. I live in New York.
   (c.) The university is in New York.

1. a. The plane is leaving Denver.
   b. I'm taking a plane.
   c. The plane leaves at 7:00 A.M.

2. a. Stores are expensive.
   b. Good vegetables are always expensive.
   c. The best vegetables are at an expensive store.

3. a. My husband made eggs.
   b. My husband made breakfast.
   c. The eggs were cold.

4. a. I sent an email.
   b. Someone wanted my bank account number.
   c. An email had my bank account number.

5. a. The hotel clerk called my wife.
   b. The speaker spoke with the hotel clerk.
   c. The hotel room is going to have a view.

□ **Exercise 29. Reading and grammar.** (Charts 12-1 → 12-6)

Part I. Answer the questions and then read the passage. Write the nouns that the pronouns refer to.

Have you ever visited or lived in another country?
What differences did you notice?
What customs did you like? What customs seemed strange to you?

An Exchange Student in Ecuador

Hiroki is from Japan. When he was sixteen, he spent four months in South America. He

stayed with a family who lived near Quito, Ecuador. Their way of life was very different from
                    1

his. At first, many things that they did and said seemed strange to Hiroki: their eating customs,
                      2

political views, ways of showing feelings, work habits, sense of humor, and more. He felt

homesick for people who were more similar to him in their customs and habits.
                3

As time went on, Hiroki began to appreciate* the way of life that his host family had.
                                4

Many activities which he did with them began to feel natural, and he developed a strong
            5

---

*appreciate = to understand a situation more completely

friendship with them. At the beginning of his stay in Ecuador, he had noticed only the customs and habits that were different between his host family and himself. At the end, he appreciated the many things which they also had in common.

        6

        7

1. who _____

2. that _____

3. who _____

4. that _____

5. which _____

6. that _____

7. which _____

Part II. Complete the sentences with information from the passage.

1. One thing that Hiroki found strange _____
_____.

2. At first, he wanted to be with people _____
_____.

3. After a while, he began to better understand _____
_____.

4. At the end of his stay, he saw many things _____
_____.

❑ **Exercise 30. Warm-up.** (Chart 12-7)
Check (✓) all the sentences that are true about the given statement.

We spoke with someone whose house burned down.

1. _____ Our house burned down.
2. _____ Another person's house burned down.
3. _____ Someone told us our house burned down.
4. _____ Someone told us their house burned down.
5. _____ Someone burned down their house.

12-7 Using *Whose* in Adjective Clauses

(a) The man called the police. **His car** ↓ **whose car** was stolen. (b) The man **whose car** *was stolen* called the police.	**Whose*** shows possession. In (a): *His car* can be changed to *whose car* to make an adjective clause. In (b): *whose car was stolen* = an adjective clause.
(c) I know a girl. **Her brother** ↓ **whose brother** is a movie star. (d) I know a girl **whose brother** *is a movie star.*	In (c): *Her brother* can be changed to *whose brother* to make an adjective clause.
(e) The people were friendly. We bought **their house.** ↓ **whose house** (f) The people **whose house** *we bought* were friendly.	In (e): *Their house* can be changed to *whose house* to make an adjective clause.

*Whose and **who's** have the same pronunciation but NOT the same meaning.
Who's = **who is**: **Who's** (*Who is*) *your teacher?*

❑ **Exercise 31. Looking at grammar.** (Chart 12-7)
Combine each pair of sentences. Follow these steps:
  (1) Underline the possessive adjective in sentence b.
  (2) Draw an arrow to the noun it refers to in sentence a.
  (3) Replace the possessive adjective with **whose**.
  (4) Place **whose** + the noun (that follows) after the noun you drew an arrow to (in Step 2).
  (5) Complete the **whose** phrase by using the rest of the words from sentence b., and make one sentence.

Examples: a. The woman is taking some time off from work.   b. Her baby is sick.
  → *The woman whose baby is sick is taking some time off from work.*

  a. The man said there isn't a lot of damage.   b. You hit his car.
  → *The man whose car you hit said there isn't a lot of damage.*

1. a. The C.E.O.* is resigning.   b. His company lost money.

2. a. Let me introduce you to the woman.   b. Her company is hiring right now.

3. a. I talked to the couple.   b. Their house was burglarized.

4. a. The child is fine.   b. You stepped on her foot.

5. a. The man is on the phone.   b. You found his cell phone.

---

*C.E.O. = chief executive officer or head of a company

❑ **Exercise 32. Let's talk: pairwork.** (Chart 12-7)
Work with a partner. Take turns changing the b. sentences to adjective clauses by combining each pair of sentences with **whose**.

SITUATION: You and your friend are at a party. You are telling your friend about the people at the party.

1. a. There is the man.   b. His car was stolen.
   → *There is the man whose car was stolen.*

2. a. There is the woman.   b. Her husband writes movie scripts.

3. a. Over there is the man.   b. His daughter is in my English class.

4. a. Over there is the woman.   b. You met her sister yesterday.

5. a. There is the professor.   b. I'm taking her course.

6. a. That is the man.   b. His daughter is a newscaster.

7. a. That is the girl.   b. I taught her brother.

8. a. There is the boy.   b. His mother is a famous musician.

❑ **Exercise 33. Listening.** (Chart 12-7)
Listen to the sentences and choose the words you hear: **who's** or **whose**.

Example: You will hear: The neighbor who's selling her house is moving overseas.
     You will choose: (who's)   whose

1. who's   whose   4. who's   whose
2. who's   whose   5. who's   whose
3. who's   whose   6. who's   whose

Exercise 34. Looking at grammar. (Chapter 12)

Work in small groups. Change a. through f. to adjective clauses. Take turns completing each sentence.

1. The man _____ is an undercover police officer.
   a. His car was stolen.
      → *The man whose car was stolen is an undercover police officer.*
   b. He invited us to his party.
   c. His son broke our car window.
   d. His dog barks all night.
   e. He is standing out in the rain.
   f. His wife is an actress.

2. The nurse _____ is leaving for a trip across the Sahara Desert.
   a. Her picture was in the paper.
   b. Her father climbed Mount Everest.
   c. She helped me when I cut myself.
   d. She works for Dr. Lang.
   e. I found her purse.
   f. I worked with her father.

3. The book _____ is very valuable.
   a. Its pages are torn.
   b. It's on the table.
   c. Sam lost it.
   d. Its cover is missing.
   e. I gave it to you.
   f. I found.

Exercise 35. Looking at grammar. (Chapter 12)

Complete the sentences with all the correct answers. Use **who, that, Ø, which, whose,** or **whom.**

1. The people ___who / that___ moved into town are Italian.

2. The lamp ___that / Ø / which___ I bought downtown is beautiful but quite expensive.

3. Everyone _____ came to the audition got a part in the play.

4. Ms. Rice is the teacher _____ class I enjoy most.

5. The man _____ I found in the doorway had collapsed from heat exhaustion.

6. I like the people with _____ I work.

7. I have a friend _____ father is a famous artist.

8. The camera _____ I bought takes very sharp pictures.

9. Students _____ have part-time jobs have to budget their time very carefully.

10. Flying squirrels _____ live in tropical rain forests stay in the trees their entire lives without ever touching the ground.

11. The people _____ car I dented were a little upset.

12. The person to _____ you should send your application is the Director of Admissions.

13. Monkeys will eat almost anything _____ they can find.

❏ **Exercise 36. Listening.** (Chapter 12)

Listen to the conversation. Complete the sentences with *that, which, whose,* or *Ø*.

Friendly advice

A: A magazine _____ I saw at the doctor's office had an article
       1

_____ you ought to read. It's about the importance of exercise in
       2

dealing with stress.

B: Why do you think I should read an article _____ deals with exercise
       3

and stress?

A: If you stop and think for a minute, you can answer that question yourself. You're under a

lot of stress, and you don't get any exercise.

B: The stress _____ I have at work doesn't bother me. It's just a normal
       4

part of my job. And I don't have time to exercise.

A: Well, you should make time. Anyone _____ job is as stressful as
       5

yours should make physical exercise part of their daily routine.

❏ **Exercise 37. Looking at grammar.** (Chapter 12)

Complete the sentences by making adjective clauses from the statements in the list. Omit the
object pronoun from the adjective clauses if possible.

> Their specialty is heart surgery.
> ✓James chose the color of paint for his bedroom walls.
> Its mouth was big enough to swallow a whole cow in one gulp.
> It erupted in Indonesia.
> His son was in an accident.
> They lived in the jungles of Southeast Asia.
> I slept on it in a hotel last night.

1. The color of paint   _James chose for his bedroom walls_   was an unusual shade of blue.

2. The man _____

   called an ambulance.

3. My back hurts today. The mattress _____

   was too soft.

4. A volcano _____ killed six people

   and damaged large areas of crops.

5. Doctors and nurses _____

   are some of the best-trained medical personnel in the world.

6. Originally, chickens were wild birds _____.

   At some point in time, humans learned how to raise them for food.

7. In prehistoric times, there was a dinosaur _____

   _____.

❏ **Exercise 38. Let's talk: interview.** (Chapter 12)
Interview your classmates. Ask two classmates each question. Share their responses with the class and see which answers are the most popular.

1. What is a dessert that you like? → *A dessert that I like is ice cream.*
2. What are some of the cities in the world you would like to visit?
3. What is one of the programs which you like to watch on TV?
4. What is one subject that you would like to know more about?
5. What are some sports you enjoy playing? watching on TV?
6. What is one of the best movies that you've ever seen?
7. What is one of the hardest classes you've ever taken?
8. Who is one of the people that you admire most in the world?

❏ **Exercise 39. Game.** (Chapter 12)
Work in teams. Answer each question with sentences that have adjective clauses. The team that has the most grammatically correct answers wins.

Example: What are the qualities of a good friend?
   → *A good friend is someone who you can depend on in times of trouble.*
   → *A good friend is a person who accepts you as you are.*
   → *A good friend is someone you can trust with secrets.*
   → *Etc.*

1. What is your idea of the ideal roommate?
2. What are the qualities of a good neighbor?
3. What kind of people make good parents?
4. What are the qualities of a good boss and a bad boss?
5. What is your idea of the ideal school?

❏ **Exercise 40. Check your knowledge.** (Chapter 12)
Edit the sentences. Correct the mistakes in adjective clauses.

1. The book that I bought it at the bookstore was very expensive.

2. The woman was nice that I met yesterday.

3. I met a woman who her husband is a famous lawyer.

4. Do you know the people who lives in that house?

5. The professor teaches Chemistry 101 is very good.

6. The people who I painted their house want me to d...

7. The people who I met them at the party last night we...

8. I enjoyed the music that we listened to it.

9. The apple tree is producing fruit that we planted it last...

10. Before I came here, I didn't have the opportunity to spea...

    language is English.

11. One thing I need to get a new alarm clock.

12. The people who was waiting to buy tickets for the game they were happy because their

    team had made it to the championship.

☐ **Exercise 41. Reading and writing.** (Chapter 12)

Part I. Read the passage and <u>underline</u> the adjective clauses.

My Friend's Vegan Diet

    I have a friend <u>who is a vegan</u>. As you may know, a vegan is a person who eats no animal products. When I first met him, I didn't understand the vegan diet. I thought *vegan* was another name for *vegetarian,* except that vegans didn't eat eggs. I soon found out I was wrong. The first time I cooked dinner for him, I made a vegetable dish which had a lot of cheese. Since cheese comes from cows, it's not vegan, so he had to scrape it off. I also served him bread that had milk in it and a dessert that was made with ice cream. Unfortunately, there wasn't much that he could eat that night. In the beginning, I had trouble thinking of meals which we could both enjoy. But he is a wonderful cook and showed me how to create delicious vegan meals. I don't know if I'll ever become a complete vegan, but I've learned a lot about the vegan diet and the delicious possibilities it has.

Part II. Write a paragraph about someone you know and something interesting or unusual about his/her life. Try to use a few adjective clauses in your paragraph.

Sample beginnings:
    I have a friend who . . . .
    I know a person who . . . .
    I've heard of a movie star who . . . .

Chapter 13

Gerunds and Infinitives

❑ **Exercise 1. Warm-up.** (Chart 13-1)
Check (✓) all the completions that are true for you.

I enjoy . . .

1. _____ traveling.
2. _____ shopping for clothes.
3. _____ playing sports.
4. _____ watching TV commercials.
5. _____ surfing the Internet.
6. _____ learning about ancient history.

13-1 Verb + Gerund

VERB GERUND (a) I *enjoy walking* in the park.	A gerund is the *-ing* form of a verb. It is used as a noun. In (a): *walking* is a gerund. It is used as the object of the verb *enjoy*.

Common Verbs Followed by Gerunds
enjoy   (b) I *enjoy working* in my garden.
finish   (c) Ann *finished studying* at midnight.
quit   (d) David *quit smoking*.
mind   (e) Would you *mind opening* the window?
postpone   (f) I *postponed doing* my homework.
put off   (g) I *put off doing* my homework.
keep (on)   (h) *Keep* (*on*) *working*. Don't stop.
consider   (i) I'*m considering going* to Hawaii.
think about   (j) I'*m thinking about going* to Hawaii.
discuss   (k) They *discussed getting* a new car.
talk about   (l) They *talked about getting* a new car.
	The verbs in the list are followed by gerunds. The list also contains phrasal verbs (e.g., *put off*) that are followed by gerunds.
	
	The verbs in the list are NOT followed by *to* + the simple form of a verb (an infinitive).
	   INCORRECT: *I enjoy to walk in the park.*
	   INCORRECT: *Bob finished to study.*
	   INCORRECT: *I'm thinking to go to Hawaii.*
	
	See Chart 2-2, p. 29, for the spelling of *-ing* verb forms.

(m) I *considered not going* to class.	Negative form: *not* + *gerund*

❑ **Exercise 2. Looking at grammar.** (Chart 13-1)
Complete each sentence with the correct form of a verb from the list.

clean	hand in	sleep
close	hire	smoke
eat	pay	work

1. The Boyds own a bakery. They work seven days a week and they are very tired. They are thinking about . . .
   a. _____ fewer hours a day.
   b. _____ their shop for a few weeks and going on vacation.
   c. _____ more workers for their shop.

2. Joseph wants to live a healthier life. He made several New Year's resolutions. For example, he has quit . . .
   a. _____ cigars
   b. _____ high-fat foods.
   c. _____ until noon on weekends.

3. Martina is a procrastinator.* She puts off . . .
   a. _____ her bills.
   b. _____ her assignments to her teacher.
   c. _____ her apartment.

❑ **Exercise 3. Looking at grammar.** (Chart 13-1)
Complete each sentence with a gerund.

1. We discussed __going / driving__ to the ocean for our vacation.

2. The Porters' car is too small for their growing family. They're considering _____ a bigger one.

3. When Martha finished _____ the floor, she dusted the furniture.

4. Beth doesn't like her job. She's talking about _____ a different job.

5. A: Are you listening to me?
   B: Yes. Keep _____. I'm listening.

6. A: Do you want to take a break?
   B: No. I'm not tired yet. Let's keep on _____ for another hour or so.

7. A: Would you mind _____ the window?
   B: No problem. I'm too hot too.

❑ **Exercise 4. Listening.** (Chart 13-1)
Complete each conversation with the words you hear. NOTE: There is a gerund in each completion.

Example: You will hear: A: I enjoy watching sports on TV, especially soccer.
                           B: Me too.

   You will write: __enjoy watching__

1. A: When you _____ your homework, could you help me in the kitchen?
   B: Sure.

*procrastinator = someone who postpones or delays doing things

2. A: Do you have any plans for this weekend?

   B: Henry and I _____ the dinosaur exhibit at the museum.

3. A: I didn't understand the answer. _____ it?

   B: I'd be happy to.

4. A: I'm _____ the meeting tomorrow.

   B: Really? Why? I hope you go. We need your input.

5. A: I've been working on this math problem for the last half hour, and I still don't understand it.

   B: Well, don't give up. _____ .

❑ **Exercise 5. Warm-up.** (Chart 13-2)
Complete the sentence using the activities in the pictures. Share your answers with a classmate. Your classmate will report a few of your answers to the class.

When I'm on vacation, I like/don't like to go _____ing.

13-2 *Go + -ing*

(a) *Did* you *go shopping* yesterday?	*Go* is followed by a gerund in certain idiomatic expressions about activities.
(b) I *went swimming* last week.	
(c) Bob *hasn't gone fishing* in years.	NOTE: There is no *to* between *go* and the gerund.
	INCORRECT: Did you go to shopping?

Common Expressions with *go* + *-ing*

go boating	go dancing	go jogging	go (window) shopping	go (water) skiing
go bowling	go fishing	go running	go sightseeing	go skydiving
go camping	go hiking	go sailing	go (ice) skating	go swimming

☐ **Exercise 6. Let's talk: pairwork.** (Chart 13-2)
Work with a partner. Take turns asking and answering questions. Use the expressions with
go + **-ing** listed in Chart 13-2.

1. Patricia often goes to the beach. She spends hours in the water. What does she like to do?
   → *She likes to go swimming.*
2. Nancy and Frank like to spend the whole day on a lake with poles in their hands. What do
   they like to do?
3. Last summer Adam went to a national park. He slept in a tent and cooked his food over a
   fire. What did Adam do last summer?
4. Tim likes to go to stores and buy things. What does he like to do?
5. Laura takes good care of her health. She runs a couple of miles every day. What does
   Laura do every day? (*There are two possible responses.*)
6. On weekends in the winter, Fred and Jean sometimes drive to a resort in the mountains.
   They like to race down the side of a mountain in the snow. What do they like to do?
7. Ivan likes to take long walks in the woods. What does Ivan like to do?
8. Sonia prefers indoor sports. She goes to a place where she rolls a 13-pound ball at some
   wooden pins. What does Sonia often do?
9. Liz and Greg know all the latest dances. What do they probably do a lot?
10. The Taylors are going to go to a little lake near their house tomorrow. The lake is
    completely frozen now that it's winter. The ice is smooth. What are the Taylors going to
    do tomorrow?
11. Mariko and Taka live near the ocean. When there's a strong wind, they like to spend the
    whole day in their sailboat. What do they like to do?
12. Tourists often get on tour buses that take them to see interesting places in an area. What
    do tourists do on these buses?
13. Colette and Ben like to jump out of airplanes. They don't open their parachutes until the
    last minute. What do they like to do?
14. What do you like to do for exercise and fun?

☐ **Exercise 7. Let's talk: interview.** (Chart 13-2)
Interview your classmates. Try to find someone who has done each activity. Make a question
for each item before you begin the interview. Share some of your answers with the class.

Find someone who . . .
1. has gone skydiving before. → *Have you gone skydiving before?*
2. likes to go waterskiing.   → *Do you like to go waterskiing?*
3. likes to go bowling.
4. goes dancing on weekends.
5. goes jogging for exercise.
6. goes fishing in the winter.
7. goes camping in the summer.
8. likes to go snow skiing.

□ **Exercise 8. Warm-up.** (Chart 13-3)
Check (✓) the sentences that are true for you.

1. _____ I hope to move to another town soon.

2. _____ I would like to get married in a few years.

3. _____ I intend to visit another country next year.

4. _____ I'm planning to become an English teacher.

13-3 Verb + Infinitive

(a) Tom *offered to lend* me some money.	Some verbs are followed by an infinitive.
(b) I've *decided to buy* a new car.	Infinitive = *to* + *the simple form of a verb*
(c) I've *decided not to keep* my old car.	Negative form: *not* + *infinitive*

Common Verbs Followed by Infinitives

want	hope	decide	seem	learn (how)
need	expect	promise	appear	try
would like	plan	offer	pretend	
would love	intend	agree		(can't) afford
	mean	refuse		(can't) wait

□ **Exercise 9. Looking at grammar.** (Chart 13-3)
Complete each sentence with the correct form of a word from the list.

be	fly to	hear	lend	visit
buy	get to	hurt	see	watch
eat	go to	leave	tell	

1. I'm planning _to fly to / to go to_ Chicago next week.

2. Hasan promised not _____ late for the wedding.

3. My husband and I would love _____ Fiji.

4. What time do you expect _____ Chicago?

5. You seem _____ in a good mood today.

6. Nadia appeared _____ asleep, but she wasn't. She was only pretending.

7. Nadia pretended _____ asleep. She pretended not _____ me when I spoke to her.

8. The Millers can't afford _____ a house.

9. My friend offered _____ me some money.

10. Tommy doesn't like broccoli. He refuses _____ it.

11. My wife and I wanted to do different things this weekend. Finally, I agreed
_____ a movie with her Saturday, and she agreed
_____ the football game with me on Sunday.

broccoli

12. I try _____ class on time every day.

13. I can't wait _____ my family again! It's been a long time.

14. I'm sorry. I didn't mean _____ you.

15. I learned how _____ time when I was six.

❏ **Exercise 10. Warm-up.** (Chart 13-4)
Check (✓) the completions that are grammatically correct.

Many children love . . .

1. _____ to eat ice cream.

2. _____ eating ice cream.

3. _____ eat ice cream.

13-4 Verb + Gerund or Infinitive

(a) It *began raining*. (b) It *began to rain*.	Some verbs are followed by either a gerund, as in (a), or an infinitive, as in (b). Usually there is no difference in meaning. Examples (a) and (b) have the same meaning.

Common Verbs Followed by Either a Gerund or an Infinitive

begin	like*	hate
start	love*	can't stand
continue		

*COMPARE: *Like* and *love* can be followed by either a gerund or an infinitive:
    I like going / to go to movies. I love playing / to play chess.
Would like and *would love* are followed by infinitives:
    I would like to go to a movie tonight. I'd love to play a game of chess right now.

❏ **Exercise 11. Looking at grammar.** (Chart 13-4)
Choose the correct verbs.

1. It started _____ around midnight.
    a. snow   (b.) snowing   (c.) to snow

2. I continued _____ even though everyone else stopped.
    a. work   b. working   c. to work

3. I like _____ emails from my friends.
    a. get   b. getting   c. to get

4. I would like _____ an email from my son who's away at college.
    a. get   b. getting   c. to get

5. I love _____ to baseball games.
    a. go   b. going   c. to go

6. I would love _____ to the baseball game tomorrow.
    a. go   b. going   c. to go

7. I hate _____ to pushy salespeople.
    a. talk   b. talking   c. to talk

8. I can't stand _____ in long lines.
    a. wait   b. waiting   c. to wait

❑ **Exercise 12. Let's talk: pairwork.** (Charts 13-1 → 13-4)
Work with a partner. Take turns combining the words in the list with the given ideas to make sentences about what you like and don't like to do.

I like	I enjoy	I hate	I don't mind
I love	I don't like	I can't stand	

1. cook
    → *I like to cook. | I like cooking. | I hate to cook. | I hate cooking. | I don't mind cooking. | I don't enjoy cooking. | Etc.*
2. live in this city
3. wash dishes
4. wait in airports
5. fly
6. eat food slowly
7. speak in front of a large group
8. drive in the city during rush hour
9. go to parties where I don't know anyone
10. listen to music while I'm trying to fall asleep
11. get in between two friends who are having an argument
12. travel to unusual places

❑ **Exercise 13. Grammar and speaking.** (Charts 13-1 → 13-4)
Complete each sentence with the infinitive or gerund form of the verb in parentheses. Then agree or disagree with the statement. Discuss your answers.

What do you do when you can't understand a native English speaker?

1. I pretend (*understand*) _____.   yes   no

2. I keep on (*listen*) _____ politely.   yes   no

3. I think, "I can't wait (*get*) _____ out of here!" OR   yes   no

"I can't wait for this person (*stop*) _____ talking."   yes   no

4. I say, "Would you mind (*repeat*) _____ that?"   yes   no

5. I begin (*nod*) _____ my head so I look like I understand.   yes   no

6. I start (*look*) _____ at my watch, so it appears I'm in a hurry.   yes   no

7. As soon as the person finishes (*speak*) _____,   yes   no
I say I have to leave.

❑ **Exercise 14. Looking at grammar.** (Charts 13-1 → 13-4)
Complete the sentences with the infinitive or gerund form of the verbs in parentheses.

1. We finished (*eat*) _____ around seven.

2. My roommate offered (*help*) _____ me with my English.

3. I'm considering (*move*) _____ to a new apartment.

4. Some children hate (*go*) _____ to school.

5. What seems (*be*) _____ the problem?

6. I don't mind (*live*) _____ with four roommates.

7. My boss refused (*give*) _____ me a raise, so I quit.

8. That's not what I meant! I meant (*say*) _____ just the opposite.

9. Julia can't stand (*sleep*) _____ in a room with all of the windows
closed.

10. Max seemed (*want*) _____ (*leave*) _____ the
party, but he kept (*talk*) _____ anyway.

11. Sam's tomato crop always failed. Finally he quit (*try*) _____ to grow
tomatoes in his garden.

□ **Exercise 15. Let's talk: pairwork.** (Charts 13-1 → 13-4)
Work with a partner. Take turns completing the sentences with **to go**/**going** + *a place*.

Example: I would like . . . .
PARTNER A: **I would like to go** to the Beach Café for dinner tonight.
PARTNER B: **I would like to go** to the movies later today.

1. I like . . . .
2. I love . . . .
3. I'd love . . . .
4. I refuse . . . .
5. I expect . . . .
6. I promised . . . .
7. I can't stand . . . .
8. I waited . . . .
9. I am thinking about . . . .
10. Are you considering . . . ?
11. I can't afford . . . .
12. Would you mind . . . ?
13. My friend and I agreed . . . .
14. I hate . . . .
15. I don't enjoy . . . .
16. My friend and I discussed . . . .
17. I've decided . . . .
18. I don't mind . . . .
19. Sometimes I put off . . . .
20. I can't wait . . . .

□ **Exercise 16. Looking at grammar.** (Charts 13-1 → 13-4)
Complete the sentences with the infinitive or gerund form of the verbs in parentheses.

1. I want (*relax*) _____ tonight.

2. I want (*stay*) _____ home and (*relax*)* _____ tonight.

3. I want (*stay*) _____ home, (*relax*) _____, and (*go*) _____ to bed early tonight.

4. I enjoy (*get*) _____ up early in the morning and (*watch*) _____ the sunrise.

5. I enjoy (*get*) _____ up early in the morning, (*watch*) _____ the sunrise, and (*listen*) _____ to the birds.

6. Mr. and Mrs. Bashir are thinking about (*sell*) _____ their old house and (*buy*) _____ a new one.

7. Kathy plans (*move*) _____ to New York City, (*find*) _____ a job, and (*start*) _____ a new life.

---

*When infinitives are connected by **and**, it is not necessary to repeat **to**.
 Example: *I need **to stay** home and (to) **study** tonight.*

350 CHAPTER 13

8. Do you like (*go*) _____ out to eat and (*let*) _____ someone else do the cooking?

9. Kevin is thinking about (*quit*) _____ his job and (*go*) _____ back to school.

10. Before you leave the office tonight, would you mind (*unplug*) _____ the coffee pot, (*turn off*) _____ all the lights, and (*lock*) _____ the door?

□ **Exercise 17. Game.** (Charts 13-1 → 13-4)
Work in teams. Your teacher will call out an item number. Make a sentence using the given words and any verb tense. Begin with **I**. The first team to come up with a grammatically correct sentence wins a point. The team with the most points wins the game.

Example: want \ go
→ *I want to go to New York City next week.*

1. plan \ go
2. consider \ go
3. offer \ help
4. like \ visit
5. enjoy \ read
6. intend \ get
7. can't afford \ buy
8. seem \ be
9. put off \ write
10. would like \ go \ swim

11. postpone \ go
12. finish \ study
13. would mind \ help
14. begin \ study
15. think about \ go
16. quit \ try
17. continue \ walk
18. learn \ speak
19. talk about \ go
20. keep \ try

□ **Exercise 18. Warm-up.** (Chart 13-5)
Agree or disagree with the statements. Notice the use of the prepositions and gerunds in green that follow the verbs.

I know someone who . . .

		yes	no
1.	never *apologizes* for being late.	yes	no
2.	is *interested* in coming to this country.	yes	no
3.	is *worried* about losing his/her job.	yes	no
4.	is *excited* about becoming a parent.	yes	no

13-5 Preposition + Gerund

(a) Kate *insisted on coming* with us.	A preposition is followed by a gerund, not an infinitive.
(b) We're *excited about going* to Tahiti.	In (a): The preposition (*on*) is followed by a gerund
(c) I *apologized for being* late.	(*coming*).

Common Expressions with Prepositions Followed by Gerunds

be afraid **of** (doing something)	be good **at**	be responsible **for**
apologize **for**	insist **on**	stop (someone) **from**
believe **in**	instead **of**	thank (someone) **for**
dream **about/of**	be interested **in**	be tired **of**
be excited **about**	look forward **to**	worry **about**/be worried **about**
feel **like**	be nervous **about**	
forgive (someone) **for**	plan **on**	

☐ **Exercise 19. Looking at grammar.** (Charts 13-5 and C-2)
Complete the sentences with a *preposition* + *gerund* and the given words.

1. I'm looking forward   +   go away for the weekend
   → I'*m looking forward* **to** *going away for the weekend.*

2. Thank you   +   hold the door open
3. I'm worried   +   be late for my appointment
4. Are you interested   +   go to the beach with us
5. I apologized   +   be late
6. Are you afraid   +   fly in small planes
7. Are you nervous   +   take your driver's test
8. We're excited   +   see the soccer game
9. Tariq insisted   +   pay the restaurant bill
10. Eva dreams   +   become a veterinarian someday
11. I don't feel   +   eat right now
12. Please forgive me   +   not write sooner
13. I'm tired   +   live with five roommates
14. I believe   +   be honest at all times
15. Let's plan   +   meet at the restaurant at six
16. Who's responsible   +   clean the classroom
17. The police stopped us +   enter the building
18. Jake's not very good +   cut his own hair

☐ **Exercise 20. Let's talk: pairwork.** (Charts 13-5 and C-2)
Work with a partner. Take turns asking and answering questions using the following pattern:
What + *the given words* + *preposition* + ***doing***.

Example: be looking forward
PARTNER A: What are you looking forward **to doing**?
PARTNER B: I'm looking forward **to going to a movie tonight**.

1. be interested		6.	be nervous
2. be worried		7.	be excited
3. thank your friend		8.	feel
4. apologize		9.	plan
5. be afraid		10.	be tired

❏ **Exercise 21. Looking at grammar.** (Charts 13-5 and C-2)
Complete each sentence with the correct preposition and the gerund form of the verb in parentheses.

1. Carlos is nervous __*about*__ (*meet*) __*meeting*__ his girlfriend's parents for the first time.

2. I believe _____ (*tell*) _____ the truth no matter what.

3. I don't go swimming in deep water because I'm afraid _____ (*drown*)
_____ .

4. Every summer, I look forward _____ (*take*) _____ a vacation with my family.

5. Do you feel _____ (*tell*) _____ me why you're so sad?

6. My father-in-law always insists _____ (*pay*) _____ for everything when we go out for dinner.

7. I want you to know that I'm sorry. I don't know if you can ever forgive me _____
(*cause*) _____ you so much trouble.

8. I'm not very good _____ (*remember*) _____ people's names.

9. How do you stop someone _____ (*do*) _____ something you know is wrong?

10. The kids are responsible _____ (*take*) _____ out the garbage.

11. Monique lost her job. That's why she is afraid _____ (*have, not*) _____
_____ enough money to pay her rent.

12. Sheila is pregnant. She's looking forward _____ (*have*) _____ another child.

13. A: I'm not happy in my work. I often dream _____ (*quit*) _____ my job.

    B: Instead _____ (*quit*) _____ your job, why don't you see if you can transfer to another department?

Listen to the conversation. Then listen again and complete the sentences with the words you hear.

A: Have you made any vacation plans?

B: Well, I _____ home because I don't like _____.
      1   2

   I hate _____ and _____ suitcases. But my wife
           3   4

   loves _____ and _____ a boat trip somewhere.
           5   6

A: So, what are you going to do?

B: Well, we couldn't agree, so we _____ home and
                                              7

   _____ tourists in our own town.
        8

A: Interesting. What are you planning _____?
                                            9

B: Well, we haven't seen the new Museum of Space yet. There's also a new art exhibit

   downtown. And my wife _____ a boat trip in
                                    10

   the harbor. Actually, when we _____ about it, we
                                          11

   discovered there were lots of things to do.

A: Sounds like a great solution!

B: Yeah, we're both really _____ more of our
                                      12

   own town.

☐ **Exercise 23. Warm-up.** (Chart 13-6)
Circle the completions that are true for you.

1. I sometimes pay for things _____.
   a. by credit card   b. by check   c. in cash

2. I usually come to school _____.
   a. by bus   b. by car   c. on foot

3. My favorite way to travel long distances is _____.
   a. by plane   b. by boat   c. by train

4. I like to communicate with my family _____.
   a. by email   b. by phone   c. in person

13-6 Using *By* and *With* to Express How Something Is Done

(a) Pat turned off the TV *by pushing* the "off" button.	*By* + *a gerund* is used to express how something is done.
(b) Mary goes to work *by bus*. (c) Andrea stirred her coffee *with a spoon*.	*By* or *with* followed by a noun is also used to express how something is done.

BY IS USED FOR MEANS OF TRANSPORTATION AND COMMUNICATION

by (air)plane	by subway*	by mail/email	by air
by boat	by taxi	by (tele)phone	by land
by bus	by train	by fax	by sea
by car	by foot (*or:* on foot)	(*but:* in person)	

OTHER USES OF *BY*

by chance	by mistake	by check (*but:* in cash)
by choice	by hand**	by credit card

WITH IS USED FOR INSTRUMENTS OR PARTS OF THE BODY
I cut down the tree *with an ax* (by using an ax).
I swept the floor *with a broom*.
She pointed to a spot on the map *with her finger*.

* *by subway* = American English; *by underground, by tube* = British English.

** The expression *by hand* is usually used to mean that something was made by a person, not by a machine: *This rug was made* ***by hand***. (A person, not a machine, made this rug.)
      COMPARE: *I touched his shoulder* ***with my hand***.

❑ **Exercise 24. Looking at grammar.** (Chart 13-6)
Complete the sentences by using *by* + *a gerund*. Use the words in the list or your own words.

eat	smile	wag	wave
drink	stay	wash	✓write
guess	take	watch	

1. Students practice written English __*by writing*__ compositions.

2. We clean our clothes _____ them in soap and water.

3. Khalid improved his English _____ a lot of TV.

4. We show other people we are happy _____ .

5. We satisfy our hunger _____ something.

6. We quench our thirst _____ something.

7. I figured out what *quench* means _____ .

8. Alex caught my attention _____ his arms in the air.

9. My dog shows me she is happy _____ her tail.

10. Carmen recovered from her cold _____ in bed and
    _____ care of herself.

☐ **Exercise 25. Looking at grammar.** (Chart 13-6)
Complete the sentences. Use **with** and words in the list.

✓a broom	a pair of scissors	a spoon
a hammer	a saw	a thermometer
a needle and thread	a shovel	

1. I swept the floor ____with a broom____.

2. I sewed a button on my shirt _____.

3. I cut the wood _____.

4. I took my temperature _____.

5. I stirred cream in my coffee _____.

6. I dug a hole in the garden _____.

7. I nailed two pieces of wood together _____.

8. I cut the paper _____.

☐ **Exercise 26. Looking at grammar.** (Chart 13-6)
Complete the sentences with **by** or **with**.

1. I opened the door ___with___ a key.

2. I went downtown ___by___ bus.

3. I dried the dishes _____ a dishtowel.

4. I went from Frankfurt to Vienna _____ train.

5. Ted drew a straight line _____ a ruler.

6. Rebecca tightened the screw in the corner of her eyeglasses _____ her fingernail.

7. I called Bill "Paul" _____ mistake.

8. I sent a copy of the contract _____ fax.

9. Talya protected her eyes from the sun _____ her hand.

10. My grandmother makes tablecloths _____ hand.

□ **Exercise 27. Warm-up.** (Chart 13-7)
Read the passage and then agree or disagree with the statements.

A White Lie

Jane gave her friend Lisa a book for her birthday. When Lisa opened it, she tried to look excited, but her husband had already given her the same book. Lisa had just finished reading it, but she thanked Jane and said she was looking forward to reading it. Lisa told a "white lie." White lies are minor or unimportant lies that a person often tells to avoid hurting someone else's feelings.

1. Telling white lies is common.	yes	no
2. It is sometimes acceptable to tell a white lie.	yes	no
3. I sometimes tell white lies.	yes	no

13-7 Using Gerunds as Subjects; Using *It* + Infinitive

(a) **Riding** horses is fun.	Examples (a) and (b) have the same meaning.
(b) **It** is fun **to ride** horses.	In (a): A gerund (**riding**) is the subject of the sentence.
	Notice: The verb (*is*) is singular because a gerund is singular.*
(c) **Coming** to class on time is important.	
(d) **It** is important **to come** to class on time.	In (b): **It** is used as the subject of the sentence. **It** has the same meaning as the infinitive phrase at the end of the sentence: **it** means **to ride horses.**

*It is also correct (but less common) to use an infinitive as the subject of a sentence: *To ride horses is fun.*

□ **Exercise 28. Grammar and speaking: pairwork.** (Chart 13-7)
Make sentences with the same meaning as the given sentences, and then decide if you agree with them. Circle *yes* or *no*. Share your answers with a partner.

Living in this town

Part I. Use a gerund as the subject.

1. It's hard to meet people here.
   → *Meeting people here is hard.*   yes   no

2. It takes time to make friends here.   yes   no

3. It is easy to get around the town.   yes   no

4. Is it expensive to live here?   yes   no

Part II. Use *it* + *an infinitive.*

5. Finding things to do on weekends is hard.
   → *It's hard to find things to do on weekends.*   yes   no

6. Walking alone at night is dangerous.   yes   no

7. Exploring this town is fun.   yes   no

8. Is finding affordable housing difficult?   yes   no

Exercise 29. Let's talk: interview. (Chart 13-7)

Interview your classmates. Ask a question and then agree or disagree with your classmate's answer. Practice using both gerunds and infinitives in your answers.

Example:
SPEAKER A (*book open*): Which is easier: to make money or to spend money?
SPEAKER B (*book closed*): It's easier to spend money than (it is) to make money.
SPEAKER A (*book open*): I agree. Spending money is easier than making money. OR
I don't agree. I think that making money is easier than spending money.

1. Which is more fun: to visit a big city or to spend time in the countryside?

2. Which is more difficult: to write English or to read English?

3. Which is easier: to understand spoken English or to speak it?

4. Which is more expensive: to go to a movie or to go to a concert?

5. Which is more comfortable: to wear shoes or to go barefoot?

6. Which is more satisfying: to give gifts or to receive them?

7. Which is more dangerous: to ride in a car or to ride in an airplane?

8. Which is more important: to come to class on time or to get an extra hour of sleep in the morning?

❏ **Exercise 30. Warm-up.** (Chart 13-8)

Agree or disagree with these statements.

In my culture . . .

		yes	no
1.	it is common for people to shake hands when they meet.	yes	no
2.	it is important for people to look one another in the eye when they are introduced.	yes	no
3.	it is strange for people to kiss one another on the cheek when they meet.	yes	no

13-8 *It* + Infinitive: Using *For* (*Someone*)

(a) *You* should study hard.	Examples (a) and (b) have a similar meaning.
(b) It is important *for you* to study hard.	Notice the pattern in (b):
(c) *Mary* should study hard.	*It is* + *adjective* + *for* (*someone*) + *infinitive phrase*
(d) It is important *for Mary* to study hard.	
(e) *We* don't have to go to the meeting.	
(f) It isn't necessary *for us* to go to the meeting.	
(g) *A dog* can't talk.	
(h) It is impossible *for a dog* to talk.	

❑ **Exercise 31. Looking at grammar.** (Chart 13-8)
Complete the sentences with the given information. Use *for* (*someone*) and an infinitive phrase in each completion.

1. Students should do their homework.

   It's really important ___for students to do their homework___.

2. Teachers should speak clearly.

   It's very important _____.

3. We don't have to hurry. There's plenty of time.

   It isn't necessary _____.

4. A fish can't live out of water for more than a few minutes.

   It's impossible _____.

5. Working parents have to budget their time carefully.

   It's necessary _____.

6. A young child usually can't sit still for a long time.

   It's difficult _____.

7. My family spends birthdays together.

   It's traditional _____.

8. My brother would love to travel to Mars someday.

   Will it be possible _____ to Mars someday?

9. I usually can't understand Mr. Alvarez. He talks too fast. How about you?

   Is it easy _____?

❑ **Exercise 32. Let's talk.** (Charts 13-7 and 13-8)
Work in small groups. Make sentences by combining the given ideas with the words in the list. Use gerunds as subjects or *it* + *an infinitive*. Share some of your sentences for other groups to agree or disagree with.

boring	embarrassing	hard	impossible	scary
dangerous	exciting	illegal	interesting	waste of time
educational	fun	important	relaxing	

Example: ride a bicycle
   → *Riding a bicycle is fun.* OR *It's fun to ride a bicycle.*

1. ride a roller coaster
2. read newspapers
3. study economics
4. drive five miles over the speed limit
5. walk in a cemetery at night
6. know the meaning of every word in a dictionary
7. never tell a lie
8. visit museums

□ **Exercise 33. Reading and grammar.** (Charts 13-7 and 13-8)
  Part I. Read the passage.

Body Language

   Different cultures use different body language. In some countries, when people meet one another, they offer a strong handshake and look the other person straight in the eye. In other countries, however, it is impolite to shake hands firmly, and it is equally rude to look a person in the eye.

   How close do people stand to another person when they are speaking to each other? This varies from country to country. In the United States and Canada, people prefer standing just a little less than an arm's length from someone. But many people in the Middle East and Latin America like moving in closer during a conversation.

   Smiling at another person is a universal, cross-cultural gesture. Although people may smile more frequently in some countries than in others, people around the world understand the meaning of a smile.

Part II. Complete the sentences with information about body language.

1. In some countries, it is important _____ .

2. In some countries, _____ is impolite.

3. In my country, _____ is important.

4. In my country, it is impolite _____ .

□ **Exercise 34. Warm-up.** (Chart 13-9)
  Check (✓) all the sentences that are grammatically correct.

   1. _____ I went to the store because I wanted to buy groceries.
   2. _____ I went to the store in order to buy groceries.
   3. _____ I went to the store to buy groceries.
   4. _____ I went to the store for groceries.
   5. _____ I went to the store for to buy groceries.

13-9 Expressing Purpose with *In Order To* and *For*

—Why did you go to the post office?	*In order to* expresses purpose. It answers the question "Why?"
(a) I went to the post office *because I wanted to mail a letter*. (b) I went to the post office *in order to* mail a letter. (c) I went to the post office *to mail* a letter.	
	In (c): *in order* is frequently omitted. Examples (a), (b), and (c) have the same meaning.
(d) I went to the post office *for* some stamps. (e) I went to the post office *to buy* some stamps. INCORRECT: *I went to the post office for to buy some stamps.* INCORRECT: *I went to the post office for buying some stamps.*	*For* is also used to express purpose, but it is a preposition and is followed by a noun phrase, as in (d).

□ **Exercise 35. Looking at grammar.** (Chart 13-9)
Make sentences by combining the phrases in Column A with those in Column B. Connect the ideas with (*in order*) *to*.

Example: I called the hotel desk . . .
→ *I called the hotel desk (in order) to ask for an extra pillow.*

Column A

1. I called the hotel desk __e__.
2. I turned on the radio _____.
3. Andy went to Egypt _____.
4. People wear boots _____.
5. I looked on the Internet _____.
6. Ms. Lane stood on her tiptoes _____.
7. The dentist moved the light closer to my face _____.
8. I clapped my hands and yelled _____.
9. Maria took a walk in the park _____.
10. I offered my cousin some money _____.

Column B

a. keep their feet warm and dry
b. reach the top shelf
c. listen to a ball game
d. find the population of Malaysia
✓e. ask for an extra pillow
f. chase a mean dog away
g. help her pay the rent
h. get some fresh air and exercise
i. see the ancient pyramids
j. look into my mouth

□ **Exercise 36. Looking at grammar.** (Chart 13-9)
Add *in order* to the sentences whenever possible.

1. I went to the bank to cash a check. → *I went to the bank in order to cash a check.*
2. I'd like to see that movie. → *(No change. The infinitive does not express purpose.)*
3. Steve went to the hospital to visit a friend.
4. I need to go to the bank today.
5. I need to go to the bank today to deposit my paycheck.
6. On my way home, I stopped at the store to buy some shampoo.
7. Masako went to the cafeteria to eat lunch.
8. Jack and Katya have decided to get married.
9. Pedro watches TV to improve his English.
10. I didn't forget to pay my rent.
11. Donna expects to graduate next spring.
12. Jerry needs to go to the bookstore to buy school supplies.

Exercise 37. Looking at grammar. (Chart 13-9)
Complete the sentences with *to* or *for*.

1. I went to Chicago ___for___ a visit.

2. I went to Chicago ___to___ visit my aunt and uncle.

3. I take long walks _____ relax.

4. I take long walks _____ relaxation.

5. I'm going to school _____ a good education.

6. I'm going to school _____ get a good education.

7. I sent a card to Carol _____ wish her a happy birthday.

8. Two police officers came to my apartment _____ ask me about a neighbor.

9. I looked on the Internet _____ information about Ecuador.

10. My three brothers, two sisters, and parents all came to town _____ my graduation.

Exercise 38. Reading and grammar. (Charts 13-1 → 13-9)
Part I. Read the passage.

Car Sharing

In hundreds of cities around the world, people can use a car without actually owning one. It's known as car sharing.

Car sharing works like this: people pay a fee to join a car-share organization. These organizations have cars available in different parts of a city 24 hours a day. Members make reservations for a car, and then go to one of several parking lots in the city to pick up the car. They pay an hourly or daily rate for driving it. They may also pay a charge for every mile/kilometer they drive. When they are finished, they return the car to a parking area for someone else to use.

Car sharing works well for several reasons. Some people only need to drive occasionally. Oftentimes, people only need a car for special occasions like moving items or taking long trips. Many people don't want the costs or responsibilities of owning a car. The car-share organization pays for gas, insurance, cleaning, and maintenance costs. Members also don't have to wait in line or fill out forms in order to get a car. They know a variety of cars will be available when they need one.

Car sharing also benefits the environment. People drive only when they need to, and fewer cars on the road means less traffic and air pollution. As more and more cities become interested in reducing traffic, car-share programs are becoming an effective alternative.

Part II. Complete the sentences with information from Part I. Use gerunds or infinitives.

1. _____ is helpful to people who don't own a car.

2. People pay a fee in order _____ a car-sharing organization.

3. Car-sharing members pay an hourly or daily rate for _____ a car.

4. Sometimes people need a car _____ furniture or to _____ a trip.

5. Many people don't want the costs of _____ a car.

Part III. Answer the questions.

1. What are three reasons that people car share?
2. What are two benefits of car sharing?
3. Does the city you live in have a form of car sharing? If yes, has it been successful? If not, why do you think there is no car-sharing program?

❑ **Exercise 39. Warm-up: pairwork.** (Chart 13-10)
Work with a partner. Read the conversation aloud and complete the sentences with the correct words in the list.

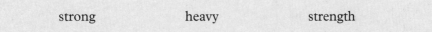

| strong | heavy | strength |

PARTNER A: Can you pick up a piano?

PARTNER B: No. It's too _____ for me to pick up. How about you?
                                    1
Can you pick up a piano?

PARTNER A: No, I'm not _____ enough to pick one up. What about the
                                    2
class? Can we pick up a piano together?

PARTNER B: Maybe. We might have enough _____ to do that as a class.
                                                                      3

13-10 Using Infinitives with *Too* and *Enough*

too + **adjective** + (**for someone**) + **infinitive**			Infinitives often follow expressions with **too**. **Too** comes in front of an adjective. In the speaker's mind, the use of **too** implies a negative result.
(a) That box is	**too** heavy		**to** lift.
(b) A piano is	**too** heavy	**for** me	**to** lift.
(c) That box is	**too** heavy	**for** Bob	**to** lift.

enough + **noun** + **infinitive**			COMPARE: *The box is too heavy. I can't lift it.* *The box is very heavy, but I can lift it.*
(d) I don't have	**enough** money	**to** buy that car.	
(e) Did you have	**enough** time	**to** finish the test?	

adjective + **enough** + **infinitive**			Infinitives often follow expressions with **enough**.
(f) Jimmy isn't	old **enough**	**to** go to school.	**Enough** comes in front of a noun.*
(g) Are you	hungry **enough**	**to** eat three sandwiches?	**Enough** follows an adjective.

*__Enough__ can also follow a noun: *I don't have **money enough** to buy that car.* In everyday English, however, **enough** usually comes in front of a noun.

□ **Exercise 40. Looking at grammar.** (Chart 13-10)
Complete the sentences with the given words. Use **too** or **enough** + *an infinitive*.

1. strong/lift   I'm not ___*strong enough to lift*___ a refrigerator.

2. weak/lift   Most people are ___*too weak to lift*___ a refrigerator without help.

3. busy/answer   I was _____ the phone. I let the call go

   to voice mail.

4. early/get   I got to the concert _____ good seats.

5. full/hold   My suitcase is _____

      _____ any more clothes.

6. large/hold   My suitcase isn't _____

   all the clothes I want to take on my trip.

7. big/get   Rex is _____

   into the doghouse.

8. big/hold   Julie's purse is _____

      _____ her dog Pepper.

❏ **Exercise 41. Looking at grammar.** (Chart 13-10)

Combine each pair of sentences.

Part I. Use *too*.

1. We can't go swimming today. It's very cold.

→ *It's **too** cold (for us) **to go** swimming today.*

2. I couldn't finish my homework last night. I was very sleepy.
3. Mike couldn't go to his aunt's housewarming party. He was very busy.
4. This jacket is very small. I can't wear it.
5. I live far from school. I can't walk there.

Part II. Use *enough*.

6. I can't reach the top shelf. I'm not that tall.

→ *I'm not tall **enough to reach** the top shelf.*

7. I can't move this furniture. I'm not that strong.
8. It's not warm today. You can't go outside without a coat.
9. I didn't stay home and miss work. I wasn't really sick, but I didn't feel good all day.

❏ **Exercise 42. Let's talk: pairwork.** (Chart 13-10)

Work with a partner. Take turns completing the sentences with infinitives.

1. I'm too short . . . .
2. I'm not tall enough . . . .
3. I'm not strong enough . . . .
4. Last night I was too tired . . . .
5. Yesterday I was too busy . . . .
6. A Mercedes-Benz is too expensive . . . .
7. I don't have enough money . . . .
8. Yesterday I didn't have enough time . . . .
9. A teenager is old enough . . . but too young . . . .
10. I know enough English . . . but not enough . . . .

❏ **Exercise 43. Looking at grammar.** (Chapter 13)

Complete each sentence with the gerund or infinitive form of the word in parentheses.

1. It's difficult for me (*remember*) __to remember__ phone numbers.

2. My cat is good at (*catch*) __catching__ mice.

3. I called my friend (*invite*) _____ her for dinner.

4. Fatima talked about (*go*) _____ to graduate school.

5. Sarosh found out what was happening by (*listen*) _____ carefully to everything that was said.

6. Michelle works 16 hours a day in order (*earn*) _____ enough money (*take*) _____ care of her elderly parents and her three children.

7. No matter how wonderful a trip is, it's always good (*get*) _____ back home and (*sleep*) _____ in your own bed.

8. I keep (*forget*) _____ to call my friend Jae. I'd better write myself a note.

9. Exercise is good for you. Why don't you walk up the stairs instead of (*use*) _____ the elevator?

❏ Exercise 44. Listening. (Chapter 13)

Listen to each item. Then listen again and complete the sentences with the words you hear.

1. My professor goes through the lecture material too quickly. It is difficult for us
_____ him. He needs _____ down and
_____ us time to understand the key points.

2. _____ others about themselves and their lives is one of the secrets of
_____ along with other people. If you want to make and
_____ friends, it is important _____ sincerely
interested in other people's lives.

3. Large bee colonies have 80,000 workers. These worker bees must visit 50 million flowers
_____ one kilogram, or 2.2 pounds, of honey. It's easy
_____ why "busy as a bee" is a common expression.

❏ Exercise 45. Reading and grammar. (Chapter 13)

Part I. Read the passage.

Uncle Ernesto

Have you ever had an embarrassing experience? My Uncle Ernesto did a few years ago while on a business trip in Norway.

Uncle Ernesto is a businessman from Buenos Aires, Argentina. He manufactures equipment for ships and needs to travel around the world to sell his products. Last year, he went to Norway to meet with a shipping company. While he was there, he found himself in an uncomfortable situation.

Uncle Ernesto was staying at a small hotel in Oslo. One morning, as he was getting ready to take a shower, he heard a knock at the door. He opened it, but no one was there. He stepped into the hallway. He still didn't see anyone, so he turned to go back to his room. Unfortunately, the door was locked. This was a big problem because he didn't have his key and he was wearing only a towel.

Instead of standing in the hallway like this, he decided to get help at the front desk and started walking toward the elevator. He hoped it would be empty, but it wasn't. He took a deep breath and got in. The other people in the elevator were surprised when they saw a man who was wrapped in a towel.

Uncle Ernesto thought about trying to explain his problem, but unfortunately he didn't know Norwegian. He knew a little English, so he said, "Door. Locked. No key." A businessman in the elevator nodded, but he wasn't smiling. Another man looked at Uncle Ernesto and smiled broadly.

The elevator seemed to move very slowly for Uncle Ernesto, but it finally reached the ground floor. He walked straight to the front desk and looked at the hotel manager helplessly. The hotel manager didn't have to understand any language to figure out the problem. He grabbed a key and led my uncle to the nearest elevator.

My uncle is still embarrassed about this incident. But he laughs a lot when he tells the story.

Part II. Check (✓) all the sentences that are grammatically correct.

1. a. _____ Uncle Ernesto went to Norway for a business meeting.
    b. _____ Uncle Ernesto went to Norway to have a business meeting.
    c. _____ Uncle Ernesto went to Norway for having a business meeting.

2. a. _____ Is necessary for him to travel in order to sell his products.
    b. _____ To sell his products, he needs to travel.
    c. _____ In order to sell his products, he needs to travel.

3. a. _____ Instead staying in the hall, he decided to get help.
    b. _____ Instead of staying in the hall, he decided to get help.
    c. _____ Instead to stay in the hall, he decided to get help.

4. a. _____ Uncle Ernesto thought about trying to explain his problem.
    b. _____ Uncle Ernesto considered about trying to explain his problem.
    c. _____ Uncle Ernesto decided not to explain his problem.

5. a. _____ It wasn't difficult for the hotel manager figuring out the problem.
    b. _____ It wasn't difficult for the hotel manager figure out the problem.
    c. _____ It wasn't difficult for the hotel manager to figure out the problem.

Exercise 46. Let's write. (Chapter 13)
Read the sample paragraph. Then write a paragraph about one of the most embarrassing experiences you have had in your life. Include some gerunds and infinitives in your writing.

Example:

My Most Embarrassing Experience

My most embarrassing experience happened at work. One morning, I was in a hurry to get to my office, so I quickly said good-bye to my wife. She knew I was planning to give an important presentation at my firm, so she wished me good luck and kissed me on the cheek. Because traffic was heavy, I got to work a few minutes after the meeting had begun. I quietly walked in and sat down. A few people looked at me strangely, but I thought it was because I was late. During my presentation, I got more stares. I began to think my presentation wasn't very good, but I continued speaking. As soon as my talk was over, I went to the restroom. When I looked in the mirror, it wasn't hard to see the problem. There was smudge of red lipstick on my cheek. I felt pretty embarrassed, but later in the day I started laughing about it and tried not to take myself so seriously.

❑ **Exercise 47. Check your knowledge.** (Chapter 13)
Edit the sentences. Correct the errors in the use of infinitives, gerunds, prepositions, and word order.

        to get
1. It is important ~~getting~~ an education.

2. I went to the bank for cashing a check.

3. Did you go to shopping yesterday?

4. I cut the rope by a knife.

5. I thanked my friend for drive me to the airport.

6. Is difficult to learn another language.

7. Timmy isn't enough old to get married.

8. Is easy this exercise to do.

9. Last night too tired no do my homework.

10. I've never gone to sailing, but I would like to.

11. Reading it is one of my hobbies.

12. The teenagers began to built a campfire to keep themselves warm.

13. Instead of settle down in one place, I'd like to travel around the world.

14. I enjoy to travel because you learn so much about other countries and cultures.

15. My grandmother likes to fishing.

16. Martina would like to has a big family.

Chapter 14

Noun Clauses

☐ **Exercise 1. Warm-up.** (Chart 14-1)
Check (✓) all the sentences that are grammatically correct.

1. _____ How much does this book cost?

2. _____ I don't know.

3. _____ How much this books costs?

4. _____ I don't know how much this book costs.

14-1 Noun Clauses: Introduction

(a) I know *his address*.
 (noun phrase)
 S V O
 	
 (b) I know *where he lives*.
 (noun clause)
 S V O
	Verbs are often followed by objects. The object is usually a noun phrase.*
	 In (a): ***his address*** is a noun phrase;
	      his address is the object of the verb *know*.
	
	 Some verbs can be followed by noun clauses.*
	 In (b): ***where he lives*** is a noun clause;
	      where he lives is the object of the verb *know*.

(c) I know *where **he lives***. S V S V O	A noun clause has its own subject and verb. In (c): ***he*** is the subject of the noun clause; ***lives*** is the verb of the noun clause.
(d) I know ***where my book is***. (noun clause)	A noun clause can begin with a question word. (See Chart 14-2.)
(e) I don't know ***if Ed is married***. (noun clause)	A noun clause can begin with *if* or ***whether***. (See Chart 14-3.)
(f) I know ***that the world is round***. (noun clause)	A noun clause can begin with ***that***. (See Chart 14-4.)

*A *phrase* is a group of related words. It does NOT contain a subject and a verb.
A *clause* is a group of related words. It contains a subject and a verb.

☐ **Exercise 2. Looking at grammar.** (Chart 14-1)
<u>Underline</u> the noun clauses. Some sentences have no noun clauses.

1. Where are the Smiths living?

2. I don't know where the Smiths are living.

3. We don't know what city they moved to.

4. We know that they moved a month ago.

5. Are they coming back?

6. I don't know if they are coming back.

❑ **Exercise 3. Warm-up: pairwork.** (Chart 14-2)
Work with a partner. Ask and answer the questions. Make true statements.

1. PARTNER A: Where do I live?
   PARTNER B: I *know / don't know* where you live.

2. PARTNER B: Where does our teacher live?
   PARTNER A: I *know / don't know* where our teacher lives.

3. PARTNER B: In your last sentence, why is "does" missing?
   PARTNER A: I *know / don't know* why "does" is missing.

4. PARTNER A: In the same sentence, why does "lives" have an "s"?
   PARTNER B: I *know / don't know* why "lives" has an "s."

14-2 Noun Clauses That Begin with a Question Word

These question words can be used to introduce a noun clause: **when, where, why, how, who, (whom), what, which, whose**.

Information Question	Noun Clause	Notice in the examples: Usual question word order is NOT used in a noun clause.
		INCORRECT: *I know where does he live.*
		CORRECT: *I know where he lives.*
Where *does he live?*	(a) I don't know *where he lives*.	
When *did they leave?*	(b) Do you know *when they left?*★	
What *did she say?*	(c) Please tell me *what she said*.	
Why *is Tom* absent?	(d) I wonder *why Tom is* absent.	
Who *is that boy?*	(e) Tell me *who that boy is*.	A noun or pronoun that follows main verb **be** in a question comes in front of **be** in a noun clause, as in (e) and (f).
Whose pen *is this?*	(f) Do you know *whose pen this is?*	
Who is in the office?	(g) I don't know *who is* in the office.	A prepositional phrase (e.g., *in the office*) does not come in front of **be** in a noun clause, as in (g) and (h).
Whose keys are on the counter?	(h) I wonder *whose keys are* on the counter.	
Who came to class?	(i) I don't know *who came* to class.	In (i) and (j): Question word order and noun clause word order are the same when the question word is used as a subject.
What happened?	(j) Tell me *what happened*.	

★A question mark is used at the end of this sentence because *Do you know* asks a question.
   Example: *Do you know when they left?*
Do you know asks a question; *when they left* is a noun clause.

□ **Exercise 4. Looking at grammar.** (Charts 5-2 and 14-2)
Decide if the given words are a noun clause or an information question. If a noun clause, add *I don't know*. If an information question, add a capital letter and a question mark.

		NOUN CLAUSE	INFORMATION QUESTION
1. a. ___I don't know___ why he left.	[x]	[ ]
b. _____ W why did he leave?	[ ]	[x]
2. a. _____ where she is living	[ ]	[ ]
b. _____ where is she living	[ ]	[ ]
3. a. _____ where did Nick go	[ ]	[ ]
b. _____ where Nick went	[ ]	[ ]
4. a. _____ what time the movie begins	[ ]	[ ]
b _____ what time does the movie begin	[ ]	[ ]
5. a. _____ why is Yoko angry	[ ]	[ ]
b. _____ why Yoko is angry	[ ]	[ ]

□ **Exercise 5. Looking at grammar.** (Charts 5-2 and 14-2)
<u>Underline</u> and identify the subject (S) and verb (V) of Speaker A's question. Complete Speaker B's response with a noun clause.

1. A: Why <u>is</u> <u>fire</u> hot?
            V S
   B: I don't know ___why fire is___ hot.

2. A: Where does Frank go to school?
   B: I don't know _____ to school.

3. A: Where did Natasha go yesterday?
   B: I don't know. Do you know _____ yesterday?

4. A: Why is Maria laughing?
   B: I don't know. Does anybody know _____?

5. A: How much does an electric car cost?
   B: Peter can tell you _____.

6. A: How long do elephants live?
   B: I don't know _____.

7. A: When was the first wheel invented?

   B: I don't know. Do you know _____?

8. A: How many hours does a light bulb burn?

   B: I don't know exactly _____.

9. A: Where did Emily buy her computer?

   B: I don't know _____.

10. A: Who lives next door to Kate?

    B: I don't know _____ next door to Kate.

11. A: Who did Julie talk to?

    B: I don't know _____ to.

12. A: Why is Mike always late?

    B: You tell me! I don't understand _____ late.

❏ **Exercise 6. Let's talk: pairwork.** (Charts 14-1 and 14-2)
Work with a partner. Take turns asking questions. Begin with ***Can you tell me***.

Questions to a teacher

1. How do I pronounce this word? → *Can you tell me how I pronounce this word?*
2. What does this mean?
3. When will I get my grades?
4. What is our next assignment?
5. How soon is the next assignment due?
6. Why is this incorrect?
7. When is a good time to meet?
8. What day does the term end?
9. Why did I fail?
10. Who will teach this class next time?

❑ **Exercise 7. Looking at grammar.** (Chart 14-2)
Complete the responses with noun clauses.

1. A: Who is that woman?
   B: I don't know *who that woman is*   .

2. A: Who is on the phone?
   B: I don't know *who is on the phone*   .

3. A: What is a lizard?
   B: I don't know _____ .

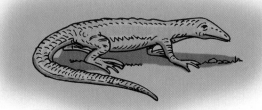

4. A: What is in that bag?
   B: I don't know _____ .

5. A: Whose car is that?
   B: I don't know _____ .

6. A: Whose car is in the driveway?
   B: I don't know _____ .

7. A: Who is Bob's doctor?
   B: I'm not sure _____ .

8. A: Whose ladder is this?
   B: I don't know _____. Hey, Hank, do you know
   _____ ?

   C: It's Hiro's.

9. A: What's at the end of a rainbow?
   B: What did you say, Susie?
   A: I want to know _____ .

❑ **Exercise 8. Let's talk: pairwork.** (Charts 14-1 and 14-2)
Work with a partner. Take turns asking questions. Begin with ***Do you know***.

Questions at home

1. Where is the phone?
2. Why is the front door open?
3. Who just called?
4. Whose socks are on the floor?

5. Why are all the lights on?
6. There's water all over the floor. What happened?
7. What did the plumber say about the broken pipe?
8. What is the repair going to cost?

❏ **Exercise 9. Looking at grammar.** (Charts 5-2 and 14-2)
Complete the sentences with the correct form of the words in parentheses.

1. A: Where (*Sophia, eat*) ___did Sophia eat___ lunch yesterday?

   B: I don't know where (*she, eat*) ___she ate___ lunch yesterday.

2. A: Do you know where (*Jason, work*) _____?

   B: Who?

   A: Jason. Where (*he, work*) _____?

   B: I don't know.

3. A: Where (*you, see*) _____ the ad for the computer sale

   last week?

   B: I don't remember where (*I, see*) _____ it. In one of the local papers,

   I think.

4. A: How can I help you?

   B: How much (*that camera, cost*) _____?

   A: You want to know how much (*this camera, cost*) _____, is that right?

   B: No, not that one. The one next to it.

5. A: How far (*you, can run*) _____ without stopping?

   B: I have no idea. I don't know how far (*I, can run*) _____

   without stopping. I've never tried.

6. A: Ann was out late last night, wasn't she? When (*she, get*) _____ in?

   B: Why do you want to know when (*she, get*) _____ home?

   A: Just curious.

7. A: What time (*it, is*) _____?

   B: I don't know. I'll ask Sara. Sara, do you know what time (*it, is*) _____?

   C: Almost four-thirty.

8. A: Mom, why (*some people, be*) _____ mean to other

   people?

   B: Honey, I don't really understand why (*some people, be*) _____

   mean to others. It's difficult to explain.

❑ **Exercise 10. Warm-up.** (Chart 14-3)
Check (✓) all the sentences that are grammatically correct.

Is Sam at work?

1. _____ I don't know if Sam is at work.

2. _____ I don't know Sam is at work.

3. _____ I don't know if Sam is at work or not.

4. _____ I don't know whether Sam is at work.

14-3 Noun Clauses That Begin with *If* or *Whether*

Yes/No Question	Noun Clause	When a yes/no question is changed to a noun clause, *if* is usually used to introduce the clause.*
Is Eric at home? Does the bus stop here? Did Alice go to Chicago?	(a) I don't know *if Eric is at home*. (b) Do you know *if the bus stops here*? (c) I wonder *if Alice went to Chicago*.	

(d) I don't know *if Eric is at home **or not***.	When *if* introduces a noun clause, the expression ***or not*** sometimes comes at the end of the clause, as in (d).
(e) I don't know ***whether** Eric is at home (or not)*.	In (e): ***whether*** has the same meaning as *if*.

*See Chart 14-10 for the use of *if* with *ask* in reported speech.

❑ **Exercise 11. Looking at grammar.** (Chart 14-3)
Change the yes/no questions to noun clauses.

1. YES/NO QUESTION: Is Carl here today?

    NOUN CLAUSE: Can you tell me ___if / whether Carl is here today___ ?

2. YES/NO QUESTION: Will Mr. Piper be at the meeting?

    NOUN CLAUSE: Do you know _____ ?

3. YES/NO QUESTION: Did Niko go to work yesterday?

    NOUN CLAUSE: I wonder _____ .

4. YES/NO QUESTION: Is there going to be a windstorm tonight?

    NOUN CLAUSE: I'm not sure _____ .

5. YES/NO QUESTION: Do you have Yung Soo's email address?

    NOUN CLAUSE: I don't know _____ .

❑ **Exercise 12. Looking at grammar.** (Chart 14-3)
Complete the noun clause in each conversation. Use *if* to introduce the noun clause.

1. A: Are you tired?

   B: Why do you want to know ___if I am___ tired?

   A: You look tired. I'm worried about you.

2. A: Are you going to be in your office later today?

   B: What? Sorry. I didn't hear you.

   A: I need to know _____ in your office later today.

3. A: Did Tim borrow my cell phone?

   B: Who?

   A: Tim. I want to know _____ my cell phone.

4. A: Can Pete watch the kids tonight?

   B: Sorry. I wasn't listening. I was thinking about something else.

   A: Have you talked to your brother Pete? We need to know _____

   _____ the kids tonight.

5. A: Are my car keys in here?

   B: Why are you asking me? How am I supposed to know _____

   _____ in here?

   A: You're sure in a bad mood, aren't you?

6. A: Does your car have a CD player?

   B: What was that?

   A: I want to know _____.

Exercise 13. Let's talk: interview. (Charts 14-2 and 14-3)

Interview your classmates. Begin your questions with ***Do you know***. Try to find people who can answer your questions.

1. What does it cost to fly from London to Paris?
2. When was this building built?
3. How far is it from Vancouver, Canada, to Riyadh, Saudi Arabia?
4. Is Australia the smallest continent?
5. How many eyes does a bat have?
6. What is one of the longest words in English?
7. Does a chimpanzee have a good memory?
8. How old is the Great Wall of China?
9. Do all birds fly?
10. Did birds come from dinosaurs?

❑ **Exercise 14. Let's talk.** (Charts 14-2 and 14-3)

Work in small groups. Choose a famous movie star or celebrity. Make complete statements using noun clauses and the given words. Share some of your sentences with the class. See if anyone knows the information.

1. What do you wonder about him/her?
   a. where → *I wonder where she lives.*
   b. what
   c. if
   d. who
   e. how
   f. why

2. What do you want to ask him/her?
   a. who → *I want to ask him who his friends are.*
   b. when
   c. what
   d. whether
   e. why
   f. where

❑ **Exercise 15. Warm-up.** (Chart 14-4)

Check (✓) the sentences that are grammatically correct. Which checked sentences do you agree with?

1. _____ I think that noun clauses are hard.
2. _____ I suppose that this chapter is useful.
3. _____ I think that some of the exercises are easy.
4. _____ Is interesting this chapter I think.

14-4 Noun Clauses That Begin with *That*

S V O (a) I think *that Mr. Jones is a good teacher.* (b) I hope *that you can come to the game.* (c) Mary realizes *that she should study harder.* (d) I dreamed *that I was on the top of a mountain.*	A noun clause can be introduced by the word ***that.*** In (a): *that Mr. Jones is a good teacher* is a noun clause. It is the object of the verb ***think.*** *That*-clauses are frequently used as the objects of verbs that express mental activity.
(e) I think *that Mr. Jones is a good teacher.* (f) I think Ø *Mr. Jones is a good teacher.*	The word ***that*** is often omitted, especially in speaking. Examples (e) and (f) have the same meaning.

Common Verbs Followed by *That*-clauses*

agree that	dream that	know that	realize that
assume that	feel that	learn that	remember that
believe that	forget that	notice that	say that
decide that	guess that	predict that	suppose that
discover that	hear that	prove that	think that
doubt that	hope that	read that	understand that

*See Appendix Chart A-4 for more verbs that can be followed by *that*-clauses.

☐ **Exercise 16. Looking at grammar.** (Chart 14-4)
Add the word ***that*** to mark the beginning of a noun clause.

           that
1. I think ∧ most people have kind hearts.

2. Last night I dreamed a monster was chasing me.

3. I believe we need to protect the rain forests.

4. Did you notice Yusef wasn't in class yesterday? I hope he's okay.

5. I trust Linda. I believe what she said. I believe she told the truth.

☐ **Exercise 17. Let's talk: pairwork.** (Chart 14-4)
Work with a partner. Take turns asking and answering questions. Use *that*-clauses. Share some of your partner's answers with the class.

1. What have you noticed about English grammar?
2. What have you heard in the news recently?
3. What did you dream recently?
4. What do you believe about people?
5. What can scientists prove?
6. What can't scientists prove?

❑ **Exercise 18. Warm-up.** (Chart 14-5)
Check (✓) the sentences that you agree with.

1. _____ I'm sure that vitamins give people more energy.

2. _____ It's true that vitamins help people live longer.

3. _____ It's a fact that vitamins help people look younger.

14-5 Other Uses of *That*-Clauses

(a) I'**m sure that** the bus stops here. (b) I'**m glad that** you're feeling better today. (c) I'**m sorry that** I missed class yesterday. (d) I **was disappointed that** you couldn't come.	*That*-clauses can follow certain expressions with **be** + *adjective* or **be** + *past participle*. The word **that** can be omitted with no change in meaning: *I'm sure Ø the bus stops here.*
(e) **It is true that** the world is round. (f) **It is a fact that** the world is round.	Two common expressions followed by *that*-clauses are: *It is true (that) . . . .* *It is a fact (that) . . . .*

Common Expressions Followed by *That*-clauses*

be afraid that	be disappointed that	be sad that	be upset that
be angry that	be glad that	be shocked that	be worried that
be aware that	be happy that	be sorry that	
be certain that	be lucky that	be sure that	It is a fact that
be convinced that	be pleased that	be surprised that	It is true that

*See Appendix Chart A-5 for more expressions that can be followed by *that*-clauses.

❑ **Exercise 19. Looking at grammar.** (Charts 14-4 and 14-5)
Add ***that*** wherever possible.

                          that
1. A: Welcome. We're glad ∧ you could come.

   B: Thank you. I'm happy to be here.

2. A: Thank you so much for your gift.

   B: I'm pleased you like it.

3. A: I wonder why Paulo was promoted to general manager instead of Andrea.

   B: So do I. I'm surprised Andrea didn't get the job. I think she is more qualified.

4. A: Are you aware you have to pass the English test to get into the university?

   B: Yes, but I'm certain I'll do well on it.

5. Are you surprised dinosaurs lived on earth for one hundred and twenty-five million (125,000,000) years?

6. Is it true human beings have lived on earth for only four million (4,000,000) years?

☐ **Exercise 20. Let's talk.** (Charts 14-4 and 14-5)
Part I. Work in small groups. Look at the health treatments below. Which ones do you know about? Which ones do you think are helpful? You may need to check your dictionary.

acupuncture	massage	naturopathy
hypnosis	meditation	yoga

Part II. Complete the sentences with words from the list. Use noun clauses. Discuss your sentences with other students.

1. I believe/think _____ is useful for _____.

2. I am certain _____.

3. I am not convinced _____.

☐ **Exercise 21. Listening and grammar.** (Charts 14-4 and 14-5)
Listen to each conversation and then complete the sentences.

Example: You will hear: MAN: I heard Jack is in jail. I can't believe it!
WOMAN: Neither can I! The police said he robbed a house.
They must have the wrong person.
You will say: a. The man is shocked that <u>Jack is in jail</u>.
b. The woman is sure that <u>the police have the wrong person</u>.

1. a. The woman thinks that . . . .
   b. The man is glad that . . . .

2. a. The mother is worried that . . . .
   b. Her son is sure that . . . .

3. a. The man is surprised that . . . .
   b. The woman is disappointed that . . . .

4. a. The man is happy that . . . .
   b. The woman is pleased that . . . .

5. a. The woman is afraid★ that . . . .
   b. The man is sure that . . . .

---

*Sometimes **be afraid** expresses fear:
I don't want to go near that dog. I'm afraid that it will bite me.
Sometimes **be afraid** expresses polite regret:
I'm afraid you have the wrong number. = I'm sorry, but I think you have the wrong number.
I'm afraid I can't come to your party. = I'm sorry, but I can't come to your party.

□ **Exercise 22. Warm-up.** (Chart 14-6)
Circle all the statements that are true for each conversation.

1. A: Did Taka remember to get food for dinner tonight?
   B: I think so.
   a. Speaker B thinks Taka got food for dinner.
   b. Speaker B is sure that Taka got food for dinner.
   c. Speaker B doesn't know for sure if Taka got food for dinner.

2. A: Is Ben marrying Tara?
   B: I hope not.
   a. Speaker B says Ben is not going to marry Tara.
   b. Speaker B doesn't know if Ben is going to marry Tara.
   c. Speaker B doesn't want Ben to marry Tara.

14-6 Substituting *So* for a *That*-Clause in Conversational Responses

(a) A: Is Ana from Peru? B: **I think so.** (*so = that Ana is from Peru*)	**Think**, **believe**, and **hope** are frequently followed by **so** in conversational English in response to a yes/no question. They are alternatives to *yes*, *no*, or *I don't know*.
(b) A: Does Judy live in Dallas? B: **I believe so.** (*so = that Judy lives in Dallas*)	**So** replaces a *that*-clause. INCORRECT: *I think so that Ana is from Peru.*
(c) A: Did you pass the test? B: **I hope so.** (*so = that I passed the test*)	
(d) A: Is Jack married? B: **I *don't* think so. / I *don't* believe so.**	Negative usage of **think so** and **believe so**: *do not think so / do not believe so*
(e) A: Did you fail the test? B: **I hope *not*.**	Negative usage of **hope** in conversational responses: *hope not*. In (e): ***I hope not*** = I hope I didn't fail the test. INCORRECT: *I don't hope so.*
(f) A: Do you want to come with us? B: Oh, I don't know. **I guess so.**	Other common conversational responses: *I guess so. I guess not.* *I suppose so. I suppose not.* NOTE: In spoken English, ***suppose*** often sounds like "spoze."

□ **Exercise 23. Looking at grammar.** (Chart 14-6)
Restate Speaker B's answers by using a *that*-clause.

1. A: Is Karen going to be home tonight?
   B: I think so.
   → *I think that Karen is going to be home tonight.*

2. A: Are we going to have a grammar test tomorrow?
    B: I don't believe so.

3. A: Will Margo be at the conference in March?
    B: I hope so.

4. A: Can horses swim?
    B: I believe so.

5. A: Do gorillas have tails?
    B: I don't think so.

6. A: Will Janet be at Omar's wedding?
    B: I suppose so.

7. A: Will your flight be canceled because of the storms?
    B: I hope not.

❑ **Exercise 24. Let's talk: pairwork.** (Chart 14-6)
Work with a partner. Take turns answering the questions. If you are not sure, use ***think so***.
If you are sure, use ***Yes*** or ***No***.

Example:
SPEAKER A (*book open*):   Does this book have more than 500 pages?
SPEAKER B (*book closed*): I think so. / I don't think so.
                            Yes, it does. / No, it doesn't.

1. Are we going to have a grammar quiz tomorrow?
2. Do spiders have noses?
3. Do spiders have eyes?
4. Is there a fire extinguisher in this room?
5. Does the word *patient* have more than one meaning?
6. Does the word *dozen* have more than one meaning?
7. Is your left foot bigger than your right foot?
8. Is there just one sun in our universe?
9. Do any English words begin with the letter "x"?
10. Do you know what a noun clause is?

❑ **Exercise 25. Warm-up.** (Chart 14-7)
Circle the quotation marks and underline the punctuation inside each quotation. What are the
differences in punctuation?

1. "Help!" Marcos yelled.

2. "Can someone help me?" he asked.

3. "I'm going to drop this box of jars," he said.

14-7 Quoted Speech

Sometimes we want to quote a speaker's words — to write a speaker's exact words. Exact quotations are used in many kinds of writing, such as newspaper articles, stories, novels, and academic papers. When we quote a speaker's words, we use quotation marks.

(a) **SPEAKERS' EXACT WORDS**	(b) **QUOTING THE SPEAKERS' WORDS**
Jane: Cats are fun to watch.	Jane said, "Cats are fun to watch."
Mike: Yes, I agree. They're graceful and playful. Do you have a cat?	Mike said, "Yes, I agree. They're graceful and playful. Do you have a cat?"

(c) HOW TO WRITE QUOTATIONS

1. Add a comma after *said.** ⟶ Jane said,
2. Add quotation marks.** ⟶ Jane said, "
3. Capitalize the first word of the quotation. ⟶ Jane said, "Cats
4. Write the quotation. Add a final period. ⟶ Jane said, "Cats are fun to watch.
5. Add quotation marks **after** the period. ⟶ Jane said, "Cats are fun to watch."

(d) Mike said, "Yes, I agree. They're graceful and playful. Do you have a cat?"	When there are two (or more) sentences in a quotation, put the quotation marks at the beginning and end of the whole quote, as in (d).
(e) INCORRECT: Mike said, "Yes, I agree." "They're graceful and playful." "Do you have a cat?"	Do NOT put quotation marks around each sentence. As with a period, put the quotation marks after a question mark at the end of a quote.
(f) "Cats are fun to watch," Jane said.	In (f): Notice that a comma (not a period) is used at the end of the QUOTED SENTENCE because ***Jane said*** comes after the quote.
(g) "Do you have a cat?" Mike asked.	In (g): Notice that a question mark (not a comma) is used at the end of the QUOTED QUESTION.

*Other common verbs besides *say* that introduce questions: *admit, announce, answer, ask, complain, explain, inquire, report, reply, shout, state, write.*

**Quotation marks are called "inverted commas" in British English.

❑ **Exercise 26. Looking at grammar.** (Chart 14-7)
Make sentences in which you quote the speaker's exact words. Use ***said*** or ***asked***. Punctuate carefully.

1. ANN: My sister is a student.

   → Ann said, "My sister is a student." OR "My sister is a student," Ann said.

2. ANN: Is your brother a student?

3. RITA: We're hungry.

4. RITA: Are you hungry too?

5. RITA: Let's eat. The food is ready.

6. JOHN F. KENNEDY: Ask not what your country can do for you. Ask what you can do for your country.

❑ **Exercise 27. Looking at grammar.** (Chart 14-7)
A teacher recently had a conversation with Roberto. Practice punctuating their quoted speech.

(TEACHER) You know sign language, don't you I asked Roberto.

(ROBERTO) Yes, I do he replied both my grandparents are deaf.

(TEACHER) I'm looking for someone who knows sign language. A deaf student is going to visit our class next Monday I said. Could you interpret for her I asked.

(ROBERTO) I'd be happy to he answered. Is she going to be a new student?

(TEACHER) Possibly I said. She's interested in seeing what we do in our English classes.

❑ **Exercise 28. Reading and writing.** (Chart 14-7)
Part I. Read the story. <u>Underline</u> the quoted speech.

The Ugly Duckling

Once upon a time, there was a mother duck. She lived on a farm and spent her days sitting on her nest of eggs. One morning, the eggs began to move and out came six little ducklings. But there was one egg that was bigger than the rest, and it didn't hatch. The mother didn't remember this egg. "I thought I had only six," she said. "But maybe I counted incorrectly."

A short time later, the seventh egg hatched. But this duckling had gray feathers, not brown like his brothers, and was quite ugly. His mother thought, "Maybe this duck isn't one of mine." He grew faster than his brothers and ate more food. He was very clumsy, and none of the other animals wanted to play with him. Much of the time he was alone.

He felt unloved by everyone, and he decided to run away from the farm. He asked other animals on the way, "Do you know of any ducklings that look like me?" But they just laughed and said, "You are the ugliest duck we have ever seen." One day, the duckling looked up and saw a group of beautiful birds overhead. They were white, with long slender necks and large wings. The duckling thought, "I want to look just like them."

He wandered alone most of the winter and finally found a comfortable bed of reeds in a pond. He thought to himself, "No one wants me. I'll just hide here for the rest of my life." There was plenty of food there, and although he was lonely, he felt a little happier.

By springtime, the duck was quite large. One morning, he saw his reflection in the water. He didn't even recognize himself. A group of swans coming back from the south saw him and flew down to the pond. "Where have you been?" they asked. "You're a swan like us." As they began to swim across the pond, a child saw them and said, "Look at the youngest swan. He's the most beautiful of all." The swan beamed with happiness, and he lived happily ever after.

Part II. Work in small groups and answer this question: What lessons does this story teach?

Part III. Write a story that includes quoted speech. Choose one of these topics:

1. Write a fable★ from your country in which animals speak.
2. Write a story that you learned when you were young.

❑ **Exercise 29. Warm-up.** (Chart 14-8)
Circle the correct words in *italics.*

Kathy and Mark said that *we / they* didn't like *our / their* new apartment.

★*a fable* = a traditional story that teaches a lesson about life

14-8 Quoted Speech vs. Reported Speech

QUOTED SPEECH (a) Ann said, "*I'm* hungry." (b) Tom said, "*I need my* pen."	QUOTED SPEECH = giving a speaker's exact words. Quotation marks are used.*
REPORTED SPEECH (c) Ann said (that) *she was* hungry. (d) Tom said (that) *he needed his* pen.	REPORTED SPEECH = giving the idea of a speaker's words. Not all of the exact words are used; pronouns and verb forms may change. Quotation marks are NOT used.* ***That*** is optional; it is more common in writing than in speaking.

Quoted speech is also called *direct speech*. *Reported speech* is also called *indirect speech*.

❑ **Exercise 30. Looking at grammar.** (Chart 14-8)
Change the pronouns from quoted speech to reported speech.

1. Mr. Smith said, "I need help with my luggage."

   → Mr. Smith said that ___*he*___ needed help with ___*his*___ luggage.

2. Mrs. Hart said, "I am going to visit my brother."

   → Mrs. Hart said that _____ was going to visit _____ brother.

3. Sergey said to me, "I will call you."

   → Sergey said _____ would call _____ .

4. Rick said to us, "I'll meet you at your house after I finish my work at my house."

   → Rick said that _____ would meet _____ at _____ house

   after _____ finished _____ work at _____ house.

❑ **Exercise 31. Warm-up.** (Chart 14-9)
Read the conversation and look at the sentences that describe it. All are correct. What difference do you notice?

JENNY: What are you doing tomorrow?
ELLA: I'm going to take my parents out to dinner.

   a. Ella said she was going to take her parents out to dinner.
   b. Ella just said she is going to take her parents out to dinner.
   c. Last week Ella said she was going to take her parents out to dinner.
   d. Ella says she is going to take her parents out to dinner.

14-9 Verb Forms in Reported Speech

(a) QUOTED: Joe said, "I *feel* good." (b) REPORTED: Joe said (that) he *felt* good. (c) QUOTED: Ken said, "I *am* happy." (d) REPORTED: Ken said (that) he *was* happy.	In formal English, if the reporting verb (e.g., *said*) is in the past, the verb in the noun clause is often also in a past form, as in (b) and (d).
— Ann said, "I am hungry." (e) — What did Ann just say? I didn't hear her. — She said (that) she *is* hungry. (f) — What did Ann say when she got home last night? — She said (that) she *was* hungry.	In informal English, often the verb in the noun clause is not changed to a past form, especially when words are reported *soon after* they are said, as in (e). In *later reporting,* however, or in formal English, a past verb is commonly used, as in (f).
(g) Ann *says* (that) she *is* hungry.	If the reporting verb is present tense (e.g., *says*), no change is made in the noun clause verb.

QUOTED SPEECH	REPORTED SPEECH (formal or later reporting)	REPORTED SPEECH (informal or immediate reporting)
He said, "I *work* hard."	He said he *worked* hard.	He said he *works* hard.
He said, "I *am working* hard."	He said he *was working* hard.	He said he *is working* hard.
He said, "I *worked* hard."	He said he *had worked* hard.	He said he *worked* hard.
He said, "I *have worked* hard."	He said he *had worked* hard.	He said he *has worked* hard.
He said, "I *am going to work* hard."	He said he *was going to work* hard.	He said he *is going to work* hard.
He said, "I *will work* hard."	He said he *would work* hard.	He said he *will work* hard.
He said, "I *can work* hard."	He said he *could work* hard.	He said he *can work* hard.

❑ **Exercise 32. Looking at grammar.** (Chart 14-9)
Complete the reported speech sentences. Use formal verb forms.

1. Sonia said, "I need some help."

   → Sonia said (that) she __*needed*__ some help.

2. Linda said, "I'm meeting David for dinner."

   → Linda said (that) she _____ David for dinner.

3. Ms. Chavez said, "I have studied in Cairo."

   → Ms. Chavez said (that) she _____ in Cairo.

4. Kazu said, "I forgot to pay my electric bill."

   → Kazu said (that) he _____ to pay his electric bill.

5. Barbara said, "I am going to fly to Hawaii for my vacation."

   → Barbara said (that) she _____ to Hawaii for her vacation.

6. I said, "I'll carry the box up the stairs."

   → I said (that) I _____ the box up the stairs.

7. Tarik said to me, "I can teach you to drive."

   → Tarik said (that) he _____ me to drive.

❑ **Exercise 33. Looking at grammar.** (Charts 14-8 and 14-9)
Change the quoted speech to reported speech. Change the verb in quoted speech to a past form in reported speech if possible.

1. Jim said, "I'm sleepy."
   → *Jim said (that) he was sleepy.*
2. Kristina said, "I don't like chocolate."
3. Carla said, "I'm planning to take a trip with my family."
4. Ahmed said, "I have already eaten lunch."
5. Kate said, "I called my doctor."
6. Mr. Rice said, "I'm going to go to Chicago."
7. Pedro said, "I will be at your house at ten."
8. Emma said, "I can't afford to buy a new car."
9. Olivia says, "I can't afford to buy a new car."
10. Ms. Acosta said, "I want to see you in my office after your meeting with your supervisor."

❑ **Exercise 34. Warm-up.** (Chart 14-10)
Circle all the sentences that are grammatically correct.

1. a. David asked Elena if she would marry him.
   b. David asked Elena would she marry him.
   c. David wanted to know if Elena would marry him.

2. a. Elena said she wasn't sure.
   b. Elena told she wasn't sure.
   c. Elena told David she wasn't sure.

14-10 Common Reporting Verbs: *Tell, Ask, Answer/Reply*

(a) Kay **said** that* she was hungry.
(b) Kay **told me** that she was hungry.
(c) Kay **told Tom** that she was hungry.
 	
  INCORRECT: *Kay told that she was hungry.*
  INCORRECT: *Kay told to me that she was hungry.*
  INCORRECT: *Kay said me that she was hungry.*
	A main verb that introduces reported speech is called a "reporting verb." **Say** is the most common reporting verb** and is usually followed immediately by a noun clause, as in (a).
	
	Tell is also commonly used. Note that **told** is followed by **me** in (b) and by **Tom** in (c).
	
	Tell needs to be followed immediately by a (pro)noun object and then by a noun clause.

(d) QUOTED: Ken asked me, "Are you tired?" REPORTED: Ken **asked** (*me*) **if** I was tired.	**Asked** is used to report questions.
(e) Ken **wanted to know if** I was tired. Ken **wondered if** I was tired. Ken **inquired whether or not** I was tired.	Questions are also reported by using **want to know**, **wonder**, and **inquire**.
(f) QUOTED: I said (to Kay), "I am not tired." REPORTED: I **answered** / **replied** that I wasn't tired.	The verbs **answer** and **reply** are often used to report replies.

*__That__ is optional. See Chapter 14-8.

Other common reporting verbs: *Kay **announced / **commented** / **complained** / **explained** / **remarked** / **stated** that she was hungry.*

□ **Exercise 35. Looking at grammar.** (Chart 14-10)
Complete the sentences with **said, told,** or **asked**.

1. Karen __told__ me that she would be here at one o'clock.

2. Jamal __said__ that he was going to get here around two.

3. Sophia __asked__ me what time I would arrive.

4. William _____ that I had a message.

5. William _____ me that someone had called me around ten-thirty.

6. I _____ William if he knew the caller's name.

7. I had a short conversation with Alice yesterday. I _____ her that I would help her move into her new apartment next week. She _____ that she would welcome the help. She _____ me if I had a truck or knew anyone who had a truck. I _____ her Dan had a truck. She _____ she would call him.

8. My uncle in Toronto called and _____ that he was organizing a surprise party for my aunt's 60th birthday. He _____ me if I could come to Toronto for the party. I _____ him that I would be happy to come. I _____ when it was. He _____ it was the last weekend in August.

□ **Exercise 36. Let's talk: pairwork.** (Charts 5-2, 14-2, 14-3, and 14-10)
Work with a partner. Write down five questions to ask your partner about his/her life or opinions. Interview your partner and write down the answers. Then report to the class some of the information you found out about your partner. Include both the question and the response. Use either formal or informal verb forms.*

Examples:
STUDENT A's question: Where were you born?
STUDENT B's response: In Nepal.
STUDENT A's report: I asked him where he was born. He said he was born in Nepal.

STUDENT B's question: Who do you admire most in the world?
STUDENT A's response: I admire my parents.
STUDENT B's report: I asked him who he admires most in the world. He said he admires his parents the most.

*In everyday spoken English, native speakers sometimes change formal/later noun clause verbs to past forms, and sometimes they don't. In an informal reporting situation such as in this exercise, either informal/immediate reporting or reporting tenses are appropriate.

☐ **Exercise 37. Looking at grammar.** (Charts 14-8 → 14-10)
Complete the paragraph based on what the people in the picture are saying. Use the formal sequence of tenses.

One day Katya and Pavel were at a restaurant. Katya picked up her menu and looked at it.

Pavel left his menu on the table. Katya asked Pavel __*what he was going to have*__. He said

_____ anything because he
　　　　　　　　　　　2

_____. He _____ already. Katya was
　　　　3　　　　　　　　　　　　　　　4

surprised. She asked him why _____. He told her
　　　　　　　　　　　　　　　　5

_____.
　　　　　　　　　　　　　　6

☐ **Exercise 38. Looking at grammar.** (Charts 14-8 → 14-10)
Change the reported speech to quoted speech. Begin a new paragraph each time the speaker changes. Pay special attention to pronouns, verb forms, and word order.

Example:
REPORTED SPEECH: This morning my mother asked me if I had gotten enough sleep last night. I told her that I was fine. I explained that I didn't need a lot of sleep. She told me that I needed to take better care of myself.

QUOTED SPEECH: *This morning my mother said, "Did you get enough sleep last night?"*
"I'm fine," I replied. "I don't need a lot of sleep."
She said, "You need to take better care of yourself."

1. In the middle of class yesterday, my friend tapped me on the shoulder and asked me what I was doing after class. I told her that I would tell her later.

2. When I was putting on my coat, Robert asked me where I was going. I told him that I had a date with Anna. He wanted to know what we were going to do. I told him that we were going to a movie.

❑ **Exercise 39. Listening.** (Charts 14-8 → 14-10)

Listen to Roger's report of his phone conversation with Angela. Then listen again and write the missing words.

Angela called and _____ me where Bill _____.
1   2

I _____ her he _____ in the lunchroom. She
3   4

_____ when he _____ back. I _____
5   6   7

he _____ back around 2:00. I _____ her if I
8   9

_____ something for her.
10

She _____ that Bill had the information she _____,
11   12

and only he _____ her. I _____ her that I
13   14

_____ him a message. She thanked me and hung up.
15

❑ **Exercise 40. Reading.** (Chapter 14)

Part I. Read the passage.

The Last Lecture

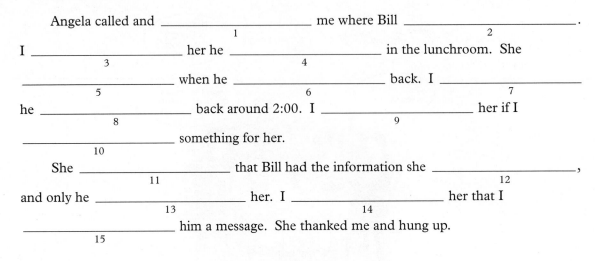

In 2007, a 47-year-old computer science professor from Carnegie Mellon University was invited to give a lecture at his university. His name was Randy Pausch, and the lecture series was called "The Last Lecture." Pausch was asked to think about what wisdom he would give to people if he knew it was his last opportunity to do so. In Pausch's case, it really was his last lecture because he had cancer and wasn't expected to survive. Pausch gave an uplifting lecture called "Really Achieving Your Childhood Dreams." The lecture was recorded and put on the Internet. A reporter for the *Wall Street Journal* was also there and wrote about it. Soon millions of people around the world heard about Pausch's inspiring talk.

Here are some quotes from Randy Pausch:

To the general public:

"Proper apologies have three parts: (1) What I did was wrong. (2) I'm sorry that I hurt you. (3) How do I make it better? It's the third part that people tend to forget."

"If I could only give three words of advice, they would be 'tell the truth.' If I got three more words, I'd add 'all the time'."

"The key question to keep asking is, 'Are you spending your time on the right things?' Because time is all you have."

"We cannot change the cards we are dealt, just how we play the hand."

To his students: "Whether you think you can or can't, you're right."

To his children: "Don't try to figure out what I wanted you to become. I want you to become what you want to become."

Sadly, in 2008, Randy Pausch died. Before his death he was able to put down his thoughts in a book, appropriately called *The Last Lecture*.

Part II. Work in small groups. Make sure the members of your group understand each quotation in Part I. Then, individually, choose one of the quotes to agree or disagree with. Use some of these phrases and support your statement with reasons.

I agree / disagree that	I think / don't think that
I believe / don't believe that	It's true that

❑ **Exercise 41. Check your knowledge.** (Chapter 14)
Edit the sentences. Correct the errors in noun clauses.

1. My friend knows where ~~do~~ I live.

2. I don't know what is your email address?

3. I think so that Mr. Lee is out of town.

4. Can you tell me that where Victor is living now?

5. I asked my uncle what kind of movies does he like.

6. I think, that my English has improved a lot.

7. Is true that people are basically the same everywhere in the world.

8. A man came to my door last week. I didn't know who is he.

9. I want to know does Pedro have a laptop computer.

10. Sam and I talked about his classes. He told that he don't like his algebra class.

11. A woman came into the room and ask me Where is your brother?

12. I felt very relieved when the doctor said, you will be fine. It's nothing serious.

13. My mother asked me that: "When you will be home?

Appendix
Supplementary Grammar Charts

UNIT A

A-1 The Present Perfect vs. The Past Perfect		
Present Perfect before now / now	(a) I am not hungry now. I **have** already **eaten**.	The PRESENT PERFECT expresses an activity that *occurred before now, at an unspecified time in the past,* as in (a).
Past Perfect before 1:00 / 1:00 P.M.	(b) I was not hungry at 1:00 P.M. I **had** already **eaten**.	The PAST PERFECT expresses an activity that *occurred before **another** time in the past.* In (b): I ate at noon. I was not hungry at 1:00 P.M. because I had already eaten before 1:00 P.M.

I laughed when I saw my son.
He **had poured** a bowl of noodles on top of his head.

A-2 The Past Progressive vs. The Past Perfect

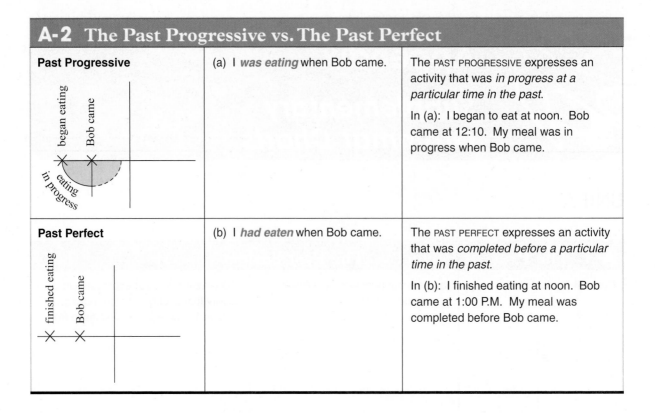

Past Progressive	(a) I *was eating* when Bob came.	The PAST PROGRESSIVE expresses an activity that was *in progress at a particular time in the past.* In (a): I began to eat at noon. Bob came at 12:10. My meal was in progress when Bob came.
Past Perfect	(b) I *had eaten* when Bob came.	The PAST PERFECT expresses an activity that was *completed before a particular time in the past.* In (b): I finished eating at noon. Bob came at 1:00 P.M. My meal was completed before Bob came.

A-3 *Still* vs. *Anymore*

Still

(a) It was cold yesterday. **It is** *still* cold today. **We** *still* **need to** wear coats. (b) The mail didn't come an hour ago. **The mail** *still* **hasn't come.**	*Still* = A situation continues to exist from past to present without change. *Still* is used in either affirmative or negative sentences. Position: midsentence*

Anymore

(c) I lived in Chicago two years ago, but then I moved to another city. **I don't live in Chicago** *anymore.*	*Anymore* = A past situation does not continue to exist at present; a past situation has changed. *Anymore* has the same meaning as *any longer*. *Anymore* is used in negative sentences. Position: end of sentence

*A midsentence adverb
   (1) precedes a simple present verb: *We* ***still need*** *to wear coats.*
   (2) follows *am, is, are, was, were*: *It* ***is still*** *cold.*
   (3) comes between a helping verb and a main verb: *Bob* ***has already arrived***.
   (4) precedes a negative helping verb: *Ann* ***still hasn't*** *come.*
   (5) follows the subject in a question: *Have* ***you already*** *seen that movie?*

A-4 Additional Verbs Followed by *That*-Clauses*

conclude that	guess that	pretend that	show that
demonstrate that	imagine that	recall that	suspect that
fear that	indicate that	recognize that	teach that
figure out that	observe that	regret that	
find out that	presume that	reveal that	

*See Chart 14-4, p. 379, for more information.

Scientists *have **concluded that*** dolphins can communicate with each other.

A-5 Additional Expressions with *Be* + *That*-Clauses*

be ashamed that	be furious that	be proud that
be amazed that	be horrified that	be terrified that
be astounded that	be impressed that	be thrilled that
be delighted that	be lucky that	
be fortunate that	be positive that	

*See Chart 14-5, p. 380, for more information.

UNIT B: Phrasal Verbs

NOTE: See the *Fundamentals of English Grammar Workbook* appendix for more practice exercises for phrasal verbs.

B-1 Phrasal Verbs

(a) We ***put off*** our trip. We'll go next month instead of this month. (*put off = postpone*)	In (a): ***put off*** = a phrasal verb A PHRASAL VERB = a verb and a particle that together have a special meaning. For example, *put off* means "postpone."
(b) Jimmy, ***put on*** your coat before you go outdoors. (*put on = place clothes on one's body*)	A PARTICLE = a "small word" (e.g., *off, on, away, back*) that is used in a phrasal verb.
(c) Someone left the scissors on the table. They didn't belong there. I ***put*** them ***away***. (*put away = put something in its usual or proper place*)	Notice that the phrasal verbs with ***put*** in (a), (b), (c), and (d) all have different meanings.
(d) After I used the dictionary, I ***put*** it ***back*** on the shelf. (*put back = return something to its original place*)	

Separable

(e) We *put **off** our trip*. = (vb + **particle** + NOUN)
(f) We *put our **trip** off*. = (vb + NOUN + **particle**)
(g) We *put **it** off*. = (vb + PRONOUN + **particle**)
	Some phrasal verbs are **separable**: a NOUN OBJECT can either
	  (1) follow the particle, as in (e), OR
	  (2) come between (separate) the verb and the particle, as in (f).
	
	If a phrasal verb is separable, a PRONOUN OBJECT comes between the verb and the particle, as in (g).
	  INCORRECT: We put off it.

Nonseparable

(h) I *ran **into** Bob*. = (vb + **particle** + NOUN)
(i) I *ran **into** him*. = (vb + **particle** + PRONOUN)
	If a phrasal verb is **nonseparable**, a NOUN or PRONOUN always follows (never precedes) the particle, as in (h) and (i).
	  INCORRECT: I ran Bob into.
	  INCORRECT: I ran him into.

Phrasal Verbs: Intransitive

(j) The machine *broke down*. (k) Please *come in*. (l) I *fell down*.	Some phrasal verbs are intransitive; i.e., they are not followed by an object.

Three-Word Phrasal Verbs

	Some two-word verbs (e.g., *drop in*) can become three-word verbs (e.g., *drop in on*).
(m) Last night some friends ***dropped in***.	In (m): ***drop in*** is not followed by an object. It is an intransitive phrasal verb (i.e., it is not followed by an object).
(n) Let's ***drop in on*** Alice this afternoon.	In (n): ***drop in on*** is a three-word phrasal verb. Three-word phrasal verbs are transitive (they are followed by objects).
(o) We *dropped in on **her*** last week.	In (o): Three-word phrasal verbs are nonseparable (the noun or pronoun follows the phrasal verb).

A **ask out** = ask (someone) to go on a date

B **blow out** = extinguish (a match, a candle)
break down = stop functioning properly
break out = happen suddenly
break up = separate, end a relationship
bring back = return
bring up = (1) raise (children)
            (2) mention, start to talk about

C **call back** = return a telephone call
call off = cancel
call on = ask (someone) to speak in class
call up = make a telephone call
cheer up = make happier
clean up = make neat and clean
come along (with) = accompany
come from = originate
come in = enter a room or building
come over (to) = visit the speaker's place
cross out = draw a line through
cut out (of) = remove with scissors or knife

D **dress up** = put on nice clothes
drop in (on) = visit without calling first or
            without an invitation
drop out (of) = stop attending (school)

E **eat out** = eat outside of one's home

F **fall down** = fall to the ground
figure out = find the solution to a problem
fill in = complete by writing in a blank space
fill out = write information on a form
fill up = fill completely with gas, water, coffee,
         etc.
find out (about) = discover information
fool around (with) = have fun while wasting
             time

G **get on** = enter a bus/an airplane/a train/a
        subway
get out of = leave a car, a taxi

get over = recover from an illness or a shock
get together (with) = join, meet
get through (with) = finish
get up = get out of bed in the morning
give away = donate, get rid of by giving
give back = return (something) to (someone)
give up = quit doing (something) or quit trying
go on = continue
go back (to) = return to a place
go out = not stay home
go over (to) = (1) approach
            (2) visit another's home
grow up (in) = become an adult

H **hand in** = give homework, test papers, etc., to
        a teacher
hand out = give (something) to this person,
        then to that person, then to
        another person, etc.
hang around/out (with) = spend time relaxing
hang up = (1) hang on a hanger or a hook
         (2) end a telephone conversation
have on = wear
help out = assist (someone)

K **keep away (from)** = not give to
keep on = continue

L **lay off** = stop employment
leave on = (1) not turn off (a light, a machine)
         (2) not take off (clothing)
look into = investigate
look over = examine carefully
look out (for) = be careful
look up = look for information in a dictionary,
        a telephone directory, an
        encyclopedia, etc.

P **pay back** = return borrowed money to
        (someone)
pick up = lift
point out = call attention to

(continued)

print out = create a paper copy from a computer

put away = put (something) in its usual or proper place

put back = return (something) to its original place

put down = stop holding or carrying

put off = postpone

put on = put clothes on one's body

put out = extinguish (stop) a fire, a cigarette

R **run into** = meet by chance

run out (of) = finish the supply of (something)

S **set out (for)** = begin a trip

shut off = stop a machine or a light, turn off

sign up (for) = put one's name on a list

show up = come, appear

sit around (with) = sit and do nothing

sit back = put one's back against a chair back

sit down = go from standing to sitting

speak up = speak louder

stand up = go from sitting to standing

start over = begin again

stay up = not go to bed

T **take back** = return

take off = (1) remove clothes from one's body
(2) ascend in an airplane

take out = invite out and pay

talk over = discuss

tear down = destroy a building

tear out (of) = remove (paper) by tearing

tear up = tear into small pieces

think over = consider

throw away/out = put in the trash, discard

try on = put on clothing to see if it fits

turn around ⎫
turn back ⎭ change to the opposite direction

turn down = decrease the volume

turn off = stop a machine or a light

turn on = start a machine or a light

turn over = turn the top side to the bottom

turn up = increase the volume

W **wake up** = stop sleeping

watch out (for) = be careful

work out = solve

write down = write a note on a piece of paper

□ **EXERCISE 1. Looking at grammar.** (Charts B-1 and B-2)
Underline the second part of the phrasal verb in each sentence.

1. I picked up a book and started to read.

2. The teacher called on me in class.

3. I get up early every day.

4. I feel okay now. I got over my cold last week.

5. I woke my roommate up when I got home.

6. I turned the radio on to listen to some music.

7. When I don't know how to spell a word, I look it up.

❑ **EXERCISE 2. Looking at grammar.** (Charts B-1 and B-2)
Check (✓) the correct sentences. In some cases, both are correct.

1. _____ I turned the light on.
   _____ I turned on the light.

2. _____ I ran into Mary.
   _____ I ran Mary into.

3. _____ Joe looked up the definition.
   _____ Joe looked the definition up.

4. _____ I took off my coat.
   _____ I took my coat off.

5. _____ I got in the car and left.
   _____ I got the car in and left.

6. _____ I figured out the answer.
   _____ I figured the answer out.

❑ **EXERCISE 3. Looking at grammar.** (Charts B-1 and B-2)
Complete the sentences with particles and the pronouns *it* or *them*. If the phrasal verb is separable, circle SEP. If it is nonseparable, circle NONSEP.

1. I got over my cold. → I got ___over it___.   SEP   (NONSEP)

2. I made up the story. → I made _____.   SEP   NONSEP

3. I put off my homework. → I put _____.   SEP   NONSEP

4. I wrote down the numbers. → I wrote _____.   SEP   NONSEP

5. I looked up the answer. → I looked _____.   SEP   NONSEP

6. I got on the bus. → I got _____.   SEP   NONSEP

7. I looked into the problem. → I looked _____.   SEP   NONSEP

8. I shut off the engine. → I shut _____.   SEP   NONSEP

9. I turned off the lights. → I turned _____.   SEP   NONSEP

10. I got off the subway. → I got _____.   SEP   NONSEP

NOTE: See the *Fundamentals of English Grammar Workbook* appendix for more practice exercises for phrasal verbs.

UNIT C: Prepositions

NOTE: See the *Fundamentals of English Grammar Workbook* appendix for practice exercises for preposition combinations.

C-1 Preposition Combinations: Introduction

ADJ + PREP (a) Ali is ***absent from*** class today. V + PREP (b) This book ***belongs to*** me.	*At, from, of, on,* and *to* are examples of prepositions. Prepositions are often combined with adjectives, as in (a), and verbs, as in (b).

C-2 Preposition Combinations: A Reference List

A
be absent from
be accustomed to
    add (*this*) to (*that*)
be acquainted with
    admire (*someone*) for (*something*)
be afraid of
    agree with (*someone*) about (*something*)
be angry at / with (*someone*) about / over (*something*)
    apologize to (*someone*) for (*something*)
    apply for (*something*)
    approve of
    argue with (*someone*) about / over (*something*)
    arrive at (*a building / a room*)
    arrive in (*a city / a country*)
    ask (*someone*) about (*something*)
    ask (*someone*) for (*something*)
be aware of

B
be bad for
    believe in
    belong to
be bored with / by
    borrow (*something*) from (*someone*)

C
be clear to
    combine with
    compare (*this*) to / with (*that*)
    complain to (*someone*) about (*something*)
be composed of
    concentrate on
    consist of
be crazy about
be crowded with
be curious about

D
    depend on (*someone*) for (*something*)
be dependent on (*someone*) for (*something*)

be devoted to
    die of / from
be different from
    disagree with (*someone*) about (*something*)
be disappointed in
    discuss (*something*) with (*someone*)
    divide (*this*) into (*that*)
be divorced from
be done with
    dream about / of
    dream of

E
be engaged to
be equal to
    escape from (*a place*)
be excited about
    excuse (*someone*) for (*something*)
    excuse from
be exhausted from

F
be familiar with
be famous for
    feel about
    feel like
    fill (*something*) with
be finished with
    forgive (*someone*) for (*something*)
be friendly to / with
be frightened of / by
be full of

G
    get rid of
be gone from
be good for
    graduate from

H
happen to
be happy about (*something*)
be happy for (*someone*)
    hear about / of (*something*) from (*someone*)
    help (*someone*) with (*something*)
    hide (*something*) from (*someone*)
    hope for
be hungry for

I
    insist on
be interested in
    introduce (*someone*) to (*someone*)
    invite (*someone*) to (*something*)
be involved in

K
be kind to
    know about

L
    laugh at
    leave for (*a place*)
    listen to
    look at
    look for
    look forward to
    look like

M
be made of
be married to
    matter to
be the matter with
    multiply (*this*) by (*that*)

N
be nervous about
be nice to

O
be opposed to

P
    pay for
be patient with
be pleased with / about
    play with
    point at
be polite to
    prefer (*this*) to (*that*)

be prepared for
    protect (*this*) from (*that*)
be proud of
    provide (*someone*) with

Q
be qualified for

R
    read about
be ready for
be related to
    rely on
be responsible for

S
be sad about
be satisfied with
be scared of / by
    search for
    separate (*this*) from (*that*)
    be similar to
    speak to / with (*someone*) about (*something*)
    stare at
    subtract (*this*) from (*that*)
be sure of / about

T
    take care of
    talk about (*something*)
    talk to / with (*someone*) about (*something*)
    tell (*someone*) about (*something*)
be terrified of / by
    thank (*someone*) for (*something*)
    think about / of
be thirsty for
be tired from
be tired of
    translate from (*one language*) to (*another*)

U
be used to

W
    wait for
    wait on
    warn about / of
    wonder about
be worried about

Listening Script

NOTE: You may want to pause the audio after each item or in longer passages so that there is enough time to complete each task.

Chapter 8: Connecting Ideas

Exercise 11, p. 213.

Paying It Forward

A few days ago, a friend and I were driving from Benton Harbor to Chicago. We didn't have any delays for the first hour, but we ran into some highway construction near Chicago. The traffic wasn't moving. My friend and I sat and waited. We talked about our jobs, our families, and the terrible traffic. Slowly it started to move.

We noticed a black sports car on the shoulder. Its blinker was on. The driver obviously wanted to get back into traffic. Car after car passed without letting him in. I decided to do a good deed, so I motioned for him to get in line ahead of me. He waved thanks, and I waved back at him.

All the cars had to stop at a toll booth a short way down the road. I held out my money to pay my toll, but the toll-taker just smiled and waved me on. She told me that the man in the black sports car had already paid my toll. Wasn't that a nice way of saying thank you?

Exercise 15, p. 215.

A strong storm

1. The noise lasted only a short time, but the wind and rain . . .
2. Some roads were under water, but ours . . .
3. Our neighbors didn't lose any trees, but we . . .
4. My son got scared, but my daughter . . .
5. My son couldn't sleep, but my daughter . . .
6. My daughter can sleep through anything, but my son . . .
7. We still need help cleaning up from the storm, but our neighbors . . .
8. We will be okay, but some people . . .

Exercise 21, p. 219.

Part I.

To get more information:

1. A: I'm going to drop this class.
   B: You are? Why? What's the matter?
2. A: My laptop doesn't have enough memory for this application.
   B: Really? Are you sure?
3. A: I can read Braille.
   B: You can? How did you learn to do that?

Part II.

To disagree:

4. A: I love this weather.
   B: I don't.
5. A: I didn't like the movie.
   B: I did!
6. A: I'm excited about graduation.
   B: I'm not.

Exercise 28, p. 223.

Understanding the Scientific Term "Matter"

The word *matter* is a chemical term. Matter is anything that has weight. This book, your finger, water, a rock, air, and the moon are all examples of matter. Heat and radio waves are not matter because they do not have weight. Happiness, dreams, and fears have no weight and are not matter.

Exercise 33, p. 225.

1. Even though I looked all over the house for my keys, . . .
2. Although it was a hot summer night, we went inside and shut the windows because . . .
3. My brother came to my graduation ceremony although . . .
4. Because the package cost so much to send, . . .
5. Even though the soccer team won the game, . . .

Chapter 9: Comparisons

Exercise 4, p. 231.

1. Lara is as old as Tanya.
2. Sylvia isn't as old as Lara.
3. Sylvia and Brigita aren't as old as Tanya.
4. Brigita isn't quite as old as Sylvia.
5. Brigita is almost as old as Sylvia.

Exercise 8, p. 234.

1. Old shoes are more comfortable for me than new shoes.
2. I like food from other countries better than food from my country.
3. Winter is more enjoyable than summer for me.
4. I am the most talkative person in my family.
5. I am the friendliest person in my family.
6. Cooked vegetables are tastier than raw vegetables.
7. Taking a bath is more relaxing than taking a shower.
8. Speaking English is the easiest of all the English skills for me.

Exercise 12, p. 237.

My family

1. My father is younger than my mother.
2. My mother is the tallest person in our family.
3. My father is a fun person to be around. He seems happy all the time.
4. My mother was happier when she was younger.
5. I have twin sisters. They are older than me.
6. I have one brother. He is the funniest person in our family.
7. He is a doctor. He works hard every day.
8. My sisters just like to have fun. I don't think they work hard at all.

Exercise 15, p. 238.

1. Frank owns a coffee shop. Business is busier this year for him than last year.
2. I've know Steven for years. He's the friendliest person I know.
3. Sam expected a hard test, but it wasn't as hard as he expected.
4. The road ends here. This is as far as we can go.
5. Jon's decision to leave his job was the worst decision he has ever made.
6. I don't know if we'll get to the theater on time, but I'm driving as fast as I can.
7. When you do the next assignment, please be more careful.
8. The dessert looks delicious, but I've eaten as much as I can.
9. It takes about an hour to drive to the airport and my flight takes an hour. So the drive takes as long as my flight.

Exercise 23, p. 242.

1. a sidewalk, a road
   a. A sidewalk is as wide as a road.
   b. A road is wider than a sidewalk.
2. a hill, a mountain
   a. A hill isn't as high as a mountain.
   b. A hill is higher than a mountain.
3. a mountain path, a mountain peak
   a. In general, hiking along a mountain path is more dangerous than climbing a mountain peak.
   b. In general, hiking along a mountain path is less dangerous than climbing a mountain peak.
4. toes, fingers
   a. Toes are longer than fingers.
   b. Fingers aren't as long as toes.
   c. Toes are shorter than fingers.
5. basic math, algebra
   a. Basic math isn't as hard as algebra.
   b. Algebra is harder than basic math.
   c. Basic math is as confusing as algebra.
   d. Basic math is less confusing than algebra.

Exercise 36, p. 249.

5. Tom has never told a funny joke.
6. Food has never tasted better.
7. I've never slept on a hard mattress.
8. I've never seen a scarier movie.

Exercise 42, p. 253.

Gold vs. Silver

Gold is similar to silver. They are both valuable metals that people use for jewelry, but they aren't the same. Gold is not the same color as silver. Gold is also different from silver in cost: gold is more expensive than silver.

Two Zebras

Look at the two zebras in the picture. Their names are Zee and Bee. Zee looks like Bee. Is Zee exactly the same as Bee? The pattern of the stripes on each zebra in the world is unique. No two zebras are exactly alike. Even though Zee and Bee are similar to each other, they are different from each other in the exact pattern of their stripes.

Chapter 10: The Passive

Exercise 3, p. 260.

An office building at night

1. The janitors clean the building at night.
   The building is cleaned by the janitors at night.
2. Window washers wash the windows.
   The windows are washed by window washers.
3. A window washer is washing a window right now.
   A window is being washed by a window washer right now.
4. The security guard has checked the offices.
   The offices have been checked by the security guard.

5. The security guard discovered an open window. An open window was discovered by the security guard.
6. The security guard found an unlocked door. An unlocked door was found by the security guard.
7. The owner will visit the building tomorrow. The building will be visited by the owner tomorrow.
8. The owner is going to announce new parking fees. New parking fees are going to be announced by the owner.

Exercise 15, p. 267.

A bike accident

A: Did you hear about the accident outside the dorm entrance?
B: No. What happened?
A: A guy on a bike was hit by a taxi.
B: Was he injured?
A: Yeah. Someone called an ambulance. He was taken to City Hospital and treated in the emergency room for cuts and bruises.
B: What happened to the taxi driver?
A: He was arrested for reckless driving.
B: He's lucky that the bicyclist wasn't killed.

Exercise 17, p. 268.

Swimming Pools

Swimming pools are very popular nowadays, but can you guess when swimming pools were first built? Was it 100 years ago? Five hundred years ago? A thousand years ago? Actually, ancient Romans and Greeks built the first swimming pools. Male athletes and soldiers swam in them for training. Believe it or not, as early as 1 B.C., a heated swimming pool was designed for a wealthy Roman. But swimming pools did not become popular until the middle of the 1800s. The city of London built six indoor swimming pools. Soon after, the modern Olympic games began, and swimming races were included in the events. After this, swimming pools became even more popular, and now they are found all over the world.

Exercise 26, p. 274.

1. When will you be done with your work?
2. I hope it's sunny tomorrow. I'm tired of this rainy weather.
3. Jason is excited about going to Hollywood.
4. Are you prepared for the driver's license test?
5. The students are involved in many school activities.
6. The kids want some new toys. They're bored with their old ones.
7. Sam is engaged to his childhood sweetheart.
8. Some animals are terrified of thunderstorms.

Exercise 28, p. 275.

1. This fruit is spoiled. I think I'd better throw it out.
2. When we got to the post office, it was closed.

3. Oxford University is located in Oxford, England.
4. Haley doesn't like to ride in elevators. She's scared of small spaces.
5. What's the matter? Are you hurt?
6. Excuse me. Could you please tell me how to get to the bus station from here? I am lost.
7. Your name is Tom Hood? Are you related to Mary Hood?
8. Where's my wallet? It's gone! Did someone take it?
9. Oh, no! Look at my sunglasses. I sat on them and now they are broken.
10. It's starting to rain. Are all of the windows shut?

Exercise 31, p. 276.

1. Jane doesn't like school because of the boring classes and assignments.
2. The store manager stole money from the cash register. His shocked employees couldn't believe it.
3. I bought a new camera. I read the directions twice, but I didn't understand them. They were too confusing for me.
4. I was out to dinner with a friend and spilled a glass of water on his pants. I felt very embarrassed, but he was very nice about it.
5. Every year for their anniversary, I surprise my parents with dinner at a different restaurant.
6. We didn't enjoy the movie. It was too scary for the kids.

Exercise 33, p. 277.

Situation: Julie was walking along the edge of the fountain outside her office building. She was with her co-worker and friend Paul. Suddenly she lost her balance and accidentally fell into the water.

1. Julie was really embarrassed.
2. Falling into the fountain was really embarrassing.
3. Her friend Paul was shocked by the sight.
4. It was a shocking sight.
5. The people around the office building were very surprised when they saw Julie in the fountain.
6. And Julie had a surprised look on her face.
7. When she fell into the fountain, some people laughed at her. It was an upsetting experience.
8. The next day Julie was a little depressed because she thought she had made a fool of herself.
9. Her friend Paul told her not to lose her sense of humor. He told her it was just another interesting experience in life.
10. He said that people were probably interested in hearing about how she fell into the fountain.

Exercise 37, p. 280.

1. In winter, the weather gets . . .
2. In summer, the weather gets . . .
3. I think I'll stop working. I'm getting . . .
4. My brother is losing some of his hair. He's getting . . .

5. Could I have a glass of water? I'm getting really . . .
6. You don't look well. Are you getting . . .

Exercise 42, p. 282.

1. What are you accustomed to doing in the evenings?
2. What time are you used to going to bed?
3. What are you accustomed to having for breakfast?
4. Are you accustomed to living in this area?
5. Do you live with someone, or do you live alone? Are you used to that?
6. Are you used to speaking English every day?
7. What are you accustomed to doing on weekends?
8. What do you think about the weather here? Are you used to it?

Exercise 51, p. 286.

1. Doctors are supposed to take good care of their patients.
2. Passengers in a car are not supposed to buckle their seat belts.
3. Teachers are supposed to help their students.
4. Airline pilots are supposed to sleep during short flights.
5. People who live in apartments are supposed to pay the rent on time.
6. A dog is not supposed to obey its master.
7. People in a movie theater are supposed to turn off their cell phones.
8. People in libraries are supposed to speak quietly.

Exercise 52, p. 286.

Zoos

Zoos are common around the world. The first zoo was established around 3,500 years ago by an Egyptian queen for her enjoyment. Five hundred years later, a Chinese emperor established a huge zoo to show his power and wealth. Later, zoos were established for the purpose of studying animals.

Zoos were supposed to take good care of animals, but some of the early ones were dark holes or dirty cages. At that time, people became disgusted with the poor care the animals were given. Later, these early zoos were replaced by scientific institutions. Animals were studied and kept in better conditions there. These research centers became the first modern zoos.

Because zoos want to treat animals well and encourage breeding, animals today are put in large, natural settings instead of small cages. They are fed a healthy diet and are watched carefully for any signs of disease. Most zoos have specially trained veterinarians and a hospital for their animals. Today, animals in these zoos are treated well, and zoo breeding programs have saved many different types of animals.

Chapter 11: Count/Noncount Nouns and Articles

Exercise 3, p. 291.

1. We have a holiday next week.
2. What are you going to do?
3. Thomas told an unusual story.
4. Thomas often tells unusual stories.
5. I have an idea!
6. Let's go shopping.
7. There's a sale on shirts and jeans.
8. Let's leave in an hour.
9. Here's a message for you.
10. You need to call your boss.

Exercise 11, p. 296.

1. At our school, teachers don't use chalk anymore.
2. Where is the soap? Did you use all of it?
3. The manager's suggestions were very helpful.
4. Which suggestion sounded best to you?
5. Is this ring made of real gold?
6. We have a lot of storms with thunder and lightning.
7. During the last storm, I found my daughter under her bed.
8. Please put the cap back on the toothpaste.
9. What do you want to do with all this stuff in the hall closet?
10. We have too much soccer and hockey equipment.

Exercise 34, p. 313.

Ice-Cream Headaches

Have you ever eaten something really cold like ice cream and suddenly gotten a headache? This is known as an "ice-cream headache." About 30 percent of the population gets this type of headache. Here is one theory about why ice-cream headaches occur. The roof of your mouth has a lot of nerves. When something cold touches these nerves, they want to warm up your brain. They make your blood vessels swell up (get bigger), and this causes a lot of pain. Ice-cream headaches generally go away after about 30–60 seconds. The best way to avoid these headaches is to keep cold food off the roof of your mouth.

Chapter 12: Adjective Clauses

Exercise 20, p. 329.

My mother's hospital stay

1. The doctor who my mother saw first spent a lot of time with her.
2. The doctor I called for a second opinion was very patient and understanding.
3. The room that my mother had was private.
4. The medicine which she took worked better than she expected.

5. The hospital that my mom chose specializes in women's care.
6. The day my mom came home happened to be her birthday.
7. I thanked the people that helped my mom.
8. The staff whom I met were all excellent.

Exercise 28, p. 334.
1. The plane which I'm taking to Denver leaves at 7:00 A.M.
2. The store that has the best vegetables is also the most expensive.
3. The eggs which my husband made for our breakfast were cold.
4. The person who sent me an email was trying to get my bank account number.
5. The hotel clerk my wife spoke with on the phone is going to give us a room with a view.

Exercise 33, p. 337.
1. I like the people whose house we went to.
2. The man whose daughter is a doctor is very proud.
3. The man who's standing by the window has a daughter at Oxford University.
4. I know a girl whose parents are both airline pilots.
5. I know a girl who's lonely because her parents travel a lot.
6. I met a 70-year-old woman who's planning to go to college.

Exercise 36, p. 339.
Friendly advice

A: A magazine that I saw at the doctor's office had an article you ought to read. It's about the importance of exercise in dealing with stress.
B: Why do you think I should read an article which deals with exercise and stress?
A: If you stop and think for a minute, you can answer that question yourself. You're under a lot of stress, and you don't get any exercise.
B: The stress that I have at work doesn't bother me. It's just a normal part of my job. And I don't have time to exercise.
A: Well, you should make time. Anyone whose job is as stressful as yours should make physical exercise part of their daily routine.

Chapter 13: Gerunds and Infinitives

Exercise 4, p. 343.
1. A: When you finish doing your homework, could you help me in the kitchen?
   B: Sure.
2. A: Do you have any plans for this weekend?
   B: Henry and I talked about seeing the dinosaur exhibit at the museum.

3. A: I didn't understand the answer. Would you mind explaining it?
   B: I'd be happy to.
4. A: I'm thinking about not attending the meeting tomorrow.
   B: Really? Why? I hope you go. We need your input.
5. A: I've been working on this math problem for the last half hour, and I still don't understand it.
   B: Well, don't give up. Keep trying.

Exercise 22, p. 354.
A: Have you made any vacation plans?
B: Well, I wanted to stay home because I don't like traveling. I hate packing and unpacking suitcases. But my wife loves to travel and wanted to take a boat trip somewhere.
A: So, what are you going to do?
B: Well, we couldn't agree, so we decided to stay home and be tourists in our own town.
A: Interesting. What are you planning to do?
B: Well, we haven't seen the new Museum of Space yet. There's also a new art exhibit downtown. And my wife would like to take a boat trip in the harbor. Actually, when we began talking about it, we discovered there were lots of things to do.
A: Sounds like a great solution!
B: Yeah, we're both really excited about seeing more of our own town.

Exercise 44, p. 366.
1. My professor goes through the lecture material too quickly. It is difficult for us to follow him. He needs to slow down and give us time to understand the key points.
2. Asking others about themselves and their lives is one of the secrets of getting along with other people. If you want to make and keep friends, it is important to be sincerely interested in other people's lives.
3. Large bee colonies have 80,000 workers. These worker bees must visit 50 million flowers to make one kilogram, or 2.2 pounds, of honey. It's easy to see why "busy as a bee" is a common expression.

Chapter 14: Noun Clauses

Exercise 21, p. 381.
1. WOMAN: My English teacher is really good. I like her a lot.
   MAN: That's great! I'm glad you're enjoying your class.

2. MOM: How do you feel, honey? You might have the flu.
   SON: I'm okay, Mom. Honest. I don't have the flu.

3. MAN: Did you really fail your chemistry course? How is that possible?

WOMAN: I didn't study hard enough. Now I won't be able to graduate on time.

4. MAN: Rachel! Hello! It's nice to see you.

WOMAN: Hi, it's nice to be here. Thank you for inviting me.

5. WOMAN: Carol has left. Look. Her closet is empty. Her suitcases are gone. She won't be back. I just know it!

MAN: She'll be back.

Exercise 39, p. 392.

Angela called and asked me where Bill was. I told her he was in the lunchroom. She asked when he would be back. I said he would be back around 2:00. I asked her if I could do something for her.

She said that Bill had the information she needed, and only he could help her. I told her that I would leave him a message. She thanked me and hung up.

Trivia Answers

Chapter 9, Exercise 7, p. 233.

1. T
2. T
3. T
4. F [The Arctic Ocean is the coldest.]
5. F [The South China Sea is the biggest.]
6. T
7. F [Asia is the largest continent in the world.]
8. T
9. F [It's South America.]
10. T

Chapter 9, Exercise 24, p. 242.

Seattle and Singapore have more rain than Manila in December.

[Manila: 58 mm. or 2.3 in.]
[Seattle: 161 mm. or 6.3 in.]
[Singapore: 306 mm. or 12 in.]

Chapter 9, Exercise 25, p. 243.

2. Indonesia has more volcanoes than Japan.
3. Saturn has more moons than Venus.
4. Sao Paulo, Brazil, has more people than New York City.
5. Finland has more islands than Greece.
6. Nepal has more mountains than Switzerland.
7. A banana has more sugar than an apple.
8. The dark meat of a chicken has more fat than the white meat of a chicken.

Chapter 9, Exercise 40, p. 251.

A: 4   D: 5
B: 50   E: 381
C: 381

Chapter 10, Exercise 10, p. 264.

3. Princess Diana was killed in a car crash in 1997.
4. Marie and Pierre Curie discovered radium.
5. Oil was discovered in Saudi Arabia in 1938.
6. Mahatma Gandhi and Martin Luther King Jr. were arrested several times for peaceful protests.
7. Michael Jackson died in 2009.
8. Leonardo da Vinci painted the Mona Lisa.
9. John F. Kennedy was elected president of the United States in 1960.

Chapter 10, Exercise 21, p. 271.

1. sand
2. whales
3. China and Mongolia
4. small spaces

Chapter 11, Exercise 37, p. 316.

1. T
2. T
3. F [Austria]
4. T
5. F
6. T
7. F [psychology/psychiatry]
8. T
9. T
10. F [The Himalayas]

Index

A/an, 290, 292, 306–307 (*Look on pages 290 and 292 and also on pages 306 through 307.*)	The numbers following the words listed in the index refer to page numbers in the text.
Full stop (period), 208*fn.* (*Look at the footnote on page 208.*)	The letters *fn.* mean "footnote." Footnotes are at the bottom of a chart or the bottom of a page.